BRAIN GAMES®

HOW TO GET AWAY WITH MURDER

pil

Publications International, Ltd.

ISBN: 978-1-64558-594-7

Manufactured in China.

8 7 6 5 4 3 2 1

Let's get social!
@Publications_International
@PublicationsInternational
@BrainGames.TM
www.pilbooks.com

CRIMINALLY
CHALLENGING PUZZLES

We're fascinated and intrigued by stories of murder—especially when the criminal got away with it. If you're a crime aficionado, this collection delivers more than 130 puzzles themed around murder and crime. Build your brain and solve an assortment of puzzles.

- See if DNA sequences are a match

- Examine photographs to spot the missing murder weapon

- Unscramble crime-themed anagrams

- Untangle cryptograms about true crimes

- Challenge your spatial skills—and flee the crime scene—as you solve mazes

- Test your observational skills with word searches

- Have fun with wordplay as you solve word ladders and "Say What" puzzles

- Test your memory against details of true crime accounts

- Use your logic skills to find the bottle with the poison, discover what gems the murderer took, and more

Some puzzles you'll solve right away. For others, you might need to set them aside for a while before returning to them. And if you get really stuck, there's always an answer key at the back. So put on your thinking cap, grab a pencil, and get started!

DNA SEQUENCE

Examine the two images below carefully. Are these sequences a match or not?

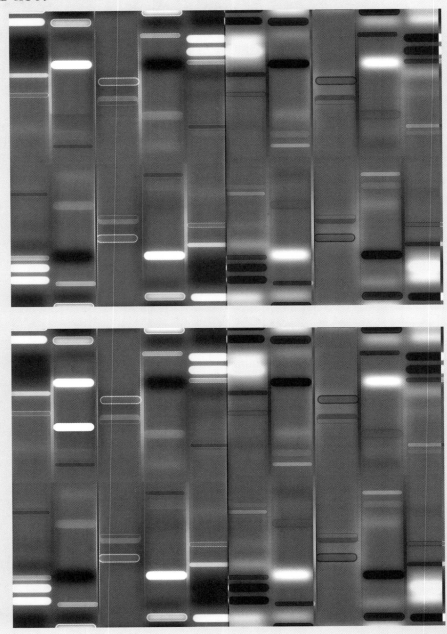

Answer on page 179.

CRIMINAL ANAGRAMS

Unscramble each word or phrase below to reveal a word or phrase related to crime.

DEAR REST   _____

RAT WARN   _____

CLOAKED WAY   _____

MEAN SIT   _____

OR SPIN   _____

DARK RILE SINS   _____

Answers on page 179.

SE7EN

Every word listed about the movie is contained within the group of letters. Words can be found in a straight line horizontally, vertically, or diagonally. They may be read either forward or backward.

DANTE	LUST
DEADLY	PRIDE
ENVY	SERIAL KILLER
GLUTTONY	SEVEN
GREED	SINS
INFERNO	SLOTH
JOHN DOE	WRATH

```
N  B  V  Z  X  Q  E  S  G  S  U  R  N  B
E  W  D  X  X  O  N  R  E  F  N  I  B  R
I  O  C  Z  C  P  V  W  H  V  H  S  E  R
H  C  D  P  R  O  Y  E  L  G  E  L  Q  G
T  L  Y  N  R  Z  E  W  D  U  L  N  L  R
A  V  N  Y  H  A  M  K  H  I  S  W  V  E
R  O  O  F  S  O  J  R  K  S  R  T  O  E
W  N  T  X  A  C  J  L  L  O  V  P  G  D
V  E  T  N  A  D  A  O  S  D  Q  S  K  X
V  E  U  U  K  I  T  J  E  F  V  D  U  E
E  G  L  N  R  H  R  A  N  L  A  H  G  M
E  Q  G  E  X  O  D  Q  W  L  S  E  G  X
U  E  S  O  S  L  A  O  P  C  A  W  Y  E
L  L  G  L  Y  D  Q  H  K  W  S  I  N  S
```

Answers on page 179.

CRIME CRYPTOGRAM

Cryptograms are messages in substitution code. Break the code to read the message. For example, THE SMART CAT might become FVO QWGDF JGF if F is substituted for T, V for H, O for E, and so on.

XLI KSPHIR WXEXI

OMPPIV GSQQMXXIH EX

PIEWX 13 QYVHIVW

FIXAIIR 1974 ERH 1986.

CRIME CRYPTOGRAM

DOHA PZ AOL WZLBKVUFT

MVY HU BUPKLUAPMLK

HTLYPJHU ZLYPHS

RPSSLY? GVKPHJ.

WHAT CHANGED? (PART 1)

Study this picture for one minute, then turn the page.

WHAT CHANGED? (PART II)

(Do not read this until you have read the previous page!)

Murder by poison! From memory, can you tell what changed between this and the previous page to pinpoint which bottle contained the poison?

Answer on page 179.

CRIME RHYMES

Each clue leads to a 2-word answer that rhymes, such as BIG PIG or STABLE TABLE. The numbers in parentheses after the clue give the number of letters in each word. For example, "cookware taken from the oven (3, 3)" would be "hot pot."

1. A blunt murder weapon found in an underground prison (8, 7): _____ in the _____

2. A sharp murder weapon hidden in a type of small flute (5, 4): _____ in the _____

3. A projectile murder weapon found hidden behind a sponge cake dessert (5, 6): _____ behind the _____

4. Projectile murder weapons hidden inside a box of these at a bakery (4, 4): _____ in the _____

5. A blunt murder weapon found wrapped inside a suit with a particular pattern (4, 9): _____ wrapped in _____

6. A blunt murder weapon discarded underneath a long seat (6, 5): _____ under a _____

7. A strangling murder weapon thrown away in a muddy area (4, 4): _____ in the _____

8. A strangling murder weapon found tucked behind a scientific device (4, 9): _____ behind the _____

Answers on page 179.

PICK YOUR
POISON

There are four bottles before you, but they've gotten jumbled up. Poison is found in one of them. If you arrange them from left to right, following the instructions given below, you will be able to know where the poison is found.

1. The poison is not found in either end bottle.

2. The blue bottle is placed somewhere to the right of the green bottle.

3. The red bottle is found to the direct left or direct right of the blue bottle.

4. The yellow bottle is to the right of the blue bottle, but not right next to it.

5. The poison is found in a color used to make the color orange.

Answers on page 179.

THE CASE OF
HAROLD SHIPMAN (PART. 1)

Read this true crime account, then turn to the next page to test your knowledge.

A very prolific serial killer in modern history was British doctor Harold Shipman, who murdered up to 400 of his patients between 1970 and 1998. Shipman was a respected member of the community, but in March 1998, a colleague became alarmed at the high death rate among his patients. She went to the local coroner, who in turn went to the police. They investigated, but found nothing out of the ordinary.

But when a woman named Kathleen Grundy died a few months later, it was revealed that she had cut her daughter Angela out of her will and, instead, allegedly bequeathed £386,000 to Shipman. Suspicious, Angela went to the police, who began another investigation. Kathleen Grundy's body was exhumed and examined, and traces of diamorphine (heroin) were found in her system. Shipman was arrested and charged with murder. When police examined his patient files more closely, they realized that Shipman was overdosing patients with diamorphine, then forging their medical records to state that they were in poor health.

Shipman was found guilty and sentenced to 15 consecutive life sentences, but he hung himself in his cell in January 2004. He did not, in the end, get away with murder.

THE CASE OF HAROLD SHIPMAN (PART I)

(Do not read this until you have read the previous page!)

1. Shipman was active between these years.

    A.   1960-1972

    B.   1971-1999

    C.   1970-1998

    D.   1984-2003

2. Grundy allegedly bequeathed this amount of money to Shipman in a suspiciously-changed will.

    A.   £386,000

    B. $386,000

    C.   £368,000

    D. $368,000

3. Shipman's killing tool, diamorphine, is most commonly known as this.

    A.   Heroin

    B.   Cocaine

    C.   Xanax

    D.   Valium

ESCAPE BY TRAIN

Run your train through the maze entering and exiting with the arrows. You can't back up, and you can't jump track at the crossovers—you must go straight through them.

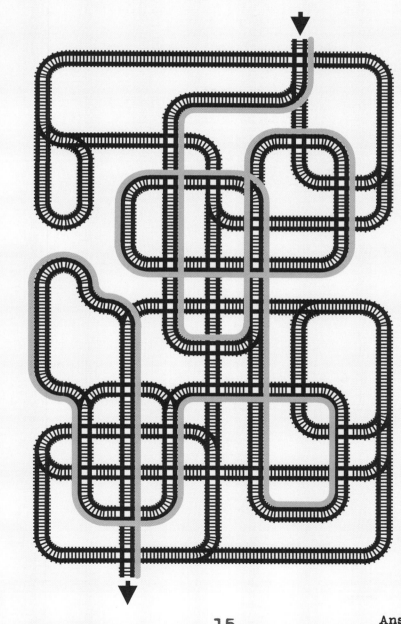

Answer on page 179.

WILL THE KILLER GO TO JAIL?

For each word ladder, change just one letter on each line to go from the top word to the bottom word. Do not change the order of the letters. You must have a common English word at each step.

KILL

_____

_____

_____

JAIL

WILL THE KILLER GO FREE?

KILL

_____

_____

_____

_____

FREE

Answers on page 180.

ZODIAC KILLER
CRYPTOGRAM

Cryptograms are messages in substitution code. Break the code to read a fact about the famous unsolved murders. For example, THE SMART CAT might become FVO QWGDF JGF if F is substituted for T, V for H, O for E, and so on

HF MSRSNO 1, 1969, OQLGG FHLOQGLF TMAYDHLFYM

FGVNIMIGLN, OQG UMAAGEH OYCGN QGLMAB, NMF

DLMFTYNTH TQLHFYTAG, MFB NMF DLMFTYNTH

GWMCYFGL MAA LGTGYUGB UYLOSMAAX YBGFOYTMA

QMFBVLYOOGF AGOOGLN OQMO THFOMYFGB TLYCG

BGOMYAN OQMO HFAX OQG KYAAGL THSAB KFHV.

GMTQ FGVNIMIGL MANH LGTGYUGB HFG OQYLB HD

M OQLGG-IMLO THBGB TYIQGL OQMO OQG VLYOGL

TAMYCGB VHSAB LGUGMA QYN YBGFOYOX. OQG

AGOOGLN MAA GFBGB VYOQ OQG NMCG NXCPHA: M

TYLTAG VYOQ M TLHNN OQLHSRQ YO.

Answers on page 180.

A GRIM VISION

Below is a group of words that, when properly arranged in the blanks, reveal a quote from Thomas Kyd.

filled mass murder world wrongs

O world, no _____ , but _____ of public _____ ,

Confused and _____ with _____ and misdeeds.

TO MURDER OR NOT TO MURDER

Below is a group of words that, when properly arranged in the blanks, reveal a quote from Shakespeare's "Hamlet."

brother's heaven murder offense primal rank

O! my _____ is _____, it smells to _____;

It hath the _____ eldest curse upon 't,

A _____ _____!

THE MURDERER'S ITINERARY

The letters in the country QATAR can be found in boxes 5, 8, 10, and 16, but not necessarily in that order. Similarly, the letters in all the other country names below can be found in the boxes indicated. Insert all the letters of the alphabet into the boxes; if you do this correctly, the shaded cells will reveal another nation that might be the murderer's location.

Hint: Look for names that share a single letter. For example, PERU shares a P with JAPAN and an R with QATAR. By comparing the number lists, you can then deduce the values of these letters.

BELGIUM: 1, 4, 7, 9, 18, 23, 24

CHILE: 4, 7, 9, 13, 21

DENMARK: 7, 8, 10, 11, 12, 17, 24

FRANCE: 7, 8, 10, 11, 21, 26

GERMANY: 1, 7, 8, 10, 11, 15, 24

HOLLAND: 9, 10, 11, 12, 13, 25

JAPAN: 10, 11, 14, 19

KUWAIT: 3, 4, 5, 10, 17, 18

LATVIA: 4, 5, 9, 10, 22

MEXICO: 4, 7, 20, 21, 24, 25

PERU: 7, 8, 14, 18

QATAR: 5, 8, 10, 16

SWEDEN: 2, 3, 7, 11, 12

ZIMBABWE: 3, 4, 6, 7, 10, 23, 24

1	2	3	4	5	6	7	8	9	10	11	12	13

14	15	16	17	18	19	20	21	22	23	24	25	26

Answers on page 180.

AN ALARMING STATISTIC

Cryptograms are messages in substitution code. Break the code to read the message. For example, THE SMART CAT might become FVO QWGDF JGF if F is substituted for T, V for H, O for E, and so on.

MR EPQSWX 15% SJ

WIVMEP QYVHIV GEWIW,

XLI ZMGXMQW EVI GLSWIR

IRXMVIPC EX VERHSQ.

COUNT TO FOUR

Cryptograms are messages in substitution code. Break the code to read the message. For example, THE SMART CAT might become FVO QWGDF JGF if F is substituted for T, V for H, O for E, and so on.

ZKDW DUH WKH IRXU

WBSHV RI KRPLFLGH?

FDSLWDO PXUGHU,

PXUGHU, PDQVODXJKWHU,

DQG FULPLQDOOB

QHJOLJHQW KRPLFLGH

PICK YOUR POISON

There are four bottles before you, but they've gotten jumbled up. Poison is found in one of them. If you arrange them from left to right, following the instructions given below, you will be able to know where the poison is found.

1. The bottles are red, yellow, green, and purple, but not necessarily in that order.

2. The second bottle from the left is the largest bottle. The smallest bottle is not right next to it.

3. The poison is not found in the smallest bottle.

4. The poison is not found in the bottle of a primary color.

5. The yellow bottle is the largest, while the green is the smallest.

6. The red bottle is not found on the end.

Answers on page 180.

MAKING A
MURDERER

Every word listed about the podcast is contained within the group of letters. Words can be found in a straight line horizontally, vertically, or diagonally. They may be read either forward or backward.

APPEALS	GUILTY
AVERY	INNOCENT
BLOOD	JUDGE
CARS	JURY
CONFESSION	LAWSUIT
DASSEY	SNOW
DNA	SUPREME COURT
EVIDENCE	WISCONSIN

```
P O B L O O D N C D R J V C
Q E U Y W L Y E S S A D O R
D H V Z T W Z W F S X N I F
Z D T I O L O W L H F B N G
U V I R D N I A O E D U N R
S J U V S E E U S T A N O H
T U S R C P N S G V F F C P
V D W A P R I C E X I P E B
S G A A N O W R E U J D N J
R E L W N D Y Z R C X U T N
A N Y K D S L J A W C S R P
C T R U O C E M E R P U S Y
W I S C O N S I N G M Y Q I
I V V U I U O X B A S R H N
```

Answers on page 180.

THE MURDEROUS
GEM THIEF

5 types of gems were stolen from the murder scene. There was 1 gem of the first type, 2 of the second type, 3 of the third type, 4 of the fourth type, and 5 of the fifth type. From the information given below, can you tell how many gemstones of each kind were taken?

1. There are fewer sapphires than pearls, but more sapphires than rubies.

2. The diamonds were not the most plentiful gem.

3. There was an odd number of pearls.

4. There was either only one emerald or only one ruby.

5. There was an odd number of sapphires.

6. There were three more pearls than rubies.

THE MOST FAMOUS UNSOLVED CASE (PART I)

Read this true crime account, then turn to the next page to test your knowledge.

In London in the late 1880s, a brutal killer known as Jack the Ripper preyed on local prostitutes. His first victim was 43-year-old Mary Ann Nichols, who was nearly decapitated during a savage knife attack. Days later, 47-year-old Annie Chapman had her organs removed from her abdomen before being left for dead. The press stirred up a wave of panic reporting that a serial killer was at large. Three weeks later, the killer was interrupted as he tore apart Swedish prostitute Elizabeth Stride. He managed to get away, only to strike again later that same night. This time the victim was Kate Eddowes. The killer, by now dubbed Jack the Ripper, removed a kidney in the process of hacking up Eddowes's body. His final kill was the most gruesome. On the night of November 9, 1888, Mary Kelly was methodically cut into pieces in an onslaught that must have lasted for several hours.

Dozens of potential Jacks have been implicated in the killings, including failed lawyer Montague John Druitt, whose body was fished out of the Thames River days after the last murder was committed. The nature of the bodily dissections has led many to conclude that Jack was a skilled physician with an advanced knowledge of anatomy. But more than a century after the savage attacks, the identity of Jack the Ripper remains a mystery. He did, in fact, get away with murder.

THE MOST FAMOUS UNSOLVED CASE (PART II)

(Do not read this until you have read the previous page!)

1. What was the name of The Ripper's first victim?

    A. Mary Ann Nichols

    B. Annie Chapman

    C. Mary Kelly

    D. Kate Eddowes

2. What was the name of his last victim?

    A. Mary Ann Nichols

    B. Annie Chapman

    C. Mary Kelly

    D. Kate Eddowes

3. Jack the Ripper operated during this decade.

    A. 1860s

    B. 1870s

    C. 1880s

    D. 1890s

ESCAPE
FROM THE PARK

Can you get away from the murder scene at the park? Start at the top left and make your way to the bottom right.

Answer on page 181.

QUOTES ON A THEME

Cryptograms are messages in substitution code. Break the code to read the message. For example, THE SMART CAT might become FVO QWGDF JGF if F is substituted for T, V for H, O for E, and so on.

OLROK UVEE BHFQ OH EVCKO;
FRLTQL BMGGHO PQ KVT EHGC.

—NKMDQNIQMLQ, "OKQ FQLBKMGO
HZ SQGVBQ"

FRLTQL, OKHRCK VO KMSQ GH
OHGCRQ, UVEE NIQMD UVOK FHNO
FVLMBREHRN HLCMG.

—NKMDQNIQMLQ, "KMFEQO"

FRLTQL UVEE HRO.

—BQLSMGOQN, "THG JRVWHOQ"

FHLTLQ UHE HRO, BQLOQXG, VO UHE
GMO ZMVEEQ.

—BKMRBQL, "OKQ BMGOQLPRLX
OMEQN"

MURDER METHOD: HIT WITH A PIPE

Change just one letter on each line to go from the top word to the bottom word. Do not change the order of the letters. You must have a common English word at each step.

HITS

___

___

PIPE

If you can't do it in three steps, try it in six!

HITS

___

___

___

___

___

PIPE

MURDER METHOD: HIT WITH A POOL CUE

Change just one letter on each line to go from the top word to the bottom word. Do not change the order of the letters. You must have a common English word at each step.

HIT

___

___

CUE

Answers on page 181.

DNA SEQUENCE

Examine the two images below carefully. Are these sequences a match or not?

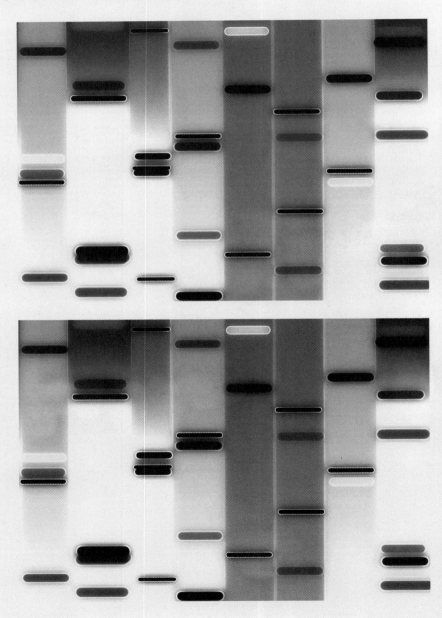

Answer on page 181.

WHAT CHANGED?.
(PART I)

Study this picture for one minute, then turn the page.

WHAT CHANGED?
(PART II)

(Do not read this until you have read the previous page!)

Murder by stabbing! From memory, can you tell what changed between this and the previous page to pinpoint which weapon was used?

Answer on page 181.

COLORFUL CRIME

Cryptograms are messages in substitution code. Break the code to read the message. For example, THE SMART CAT might become FVO QWGDF JGF if F is substituted for T, V for H, O for E, and so on.

"GSHKX GRKXZY" GXK

SKYYGMKY ZNGZ MU UAZ ZU

ZNK VAHROI KBKXE ZOSK G

INORJ MUKY SOYYOTM.

CRIME CRYPTOGRAM

Cryptograms are messages in substitution code. Break the code to read the message. For example, THE SMART CAT might become FVO QWGDF JGF if F is substituted for T, V for H, O for E, and so on.

JUB JRER GUR UVYYFVQR

FGENATYREF? NATRYB OHBAB

WE. NAQ XRAARGU OVNAPUV.

33   Answers on page 181.

PICK YOUR POISON

There are four bottles before you, but they've gotten jumbled up. Poison is found in one of them. If you arrange them from left to right, following the instructions given below, you will be able to know where the poison is found.

1. Two bottles are blue, and they are not next to each other.

2. The green bottle is either the second bottle from the left or the bottle at the far right.

3. The poison is in the bottle between the two bottles of the same color.

4. The green bottle is not next to the bottle with the poison nor does it contain the poison.

5. The yellow bottle is not next to the green bottle.

Answers on page 181.

ROMANCE
GONE WRONG

Change just one letter on each line to go from the top word to the bottom word. Do not change the order of the letters. You must have a common English word at each step.

KISS

——

——

——

——

——

——

KILL

 Answers on page 181.

ONE WAY TO END A MARRIAGE

Below is a group of words that, when properly arranged in the blanks, reveal a quote from Homer.

contrived deeds foul heart nothing plotted
shameless woman

There is _____ more dread and more _____
than a _____ who plans such _____ in her
_____ as the _____ deed which she _____
when she _____ her husband's murder.

A NOISY CRIME

Below is a group of words that, when properly arranged in the blanks, reveal a quote from John Webster.

other sins shrieks speak

_____ _____ only _____; murder _____ out.

THE CASE OF
ANDREI CHIKATILO (PART I)

Read this true crime account, then turn to the next page to test your knowledge.

Andrei Chikatilo was Russia's most notorious serial killer. The Rostov Ripper, as he came to be called (Rostov was the oblast in which he committed his crimes), began his rampage in 1978 in the city of Shakhty, where he started abducting teenagers and subjecting them to unspeakable torture before raping and murdering them, and, often, cannibalizing their bodies. Authorities gave the crimes little attention, but as the body count grew, police were forced to face the facts—Russia had a serial killer.

Chikatilo was actually brought in for questioning when the police found a rope and butcher knife in his bag during a routine search, but he was released and allowed to continue his killing spree. In the end, he got careless and was arrested near the scene of his latest murder. Under interrogation, he confessed to 56 murders. During the trial, he was kept in a cage in the middle of the court, playing up the image of the deranged lunatic. It didn't help his cause, though. He was found guilty and executed with a shot to the back of the head on February 14, 1994. In the end, he did not get away with murder.

THE CASE OF
ANDREI CHIKATILO (PART II)

(Do not read this until you have read the previous page!)

1. What nickname was given to Chikatilo?

   A. The Shakhty Strangler

   B. The Russian Ripper

   C. The Soviet Serial Killer

   D. The Rostov Ripper

2. Chikatilo committed at least this many murders.

   A. 30

   B. 40

   C. 55

   D. 100

3. Police found these in a bag during a search.

   A. Rope and butcher knife

   B. Wrench and butcher knife

   C. Rope and crowbar

   D. Sword and spear

Answers on page 181.

CRIMINAL ANAGRAMS

Unscramble each word or phrase below to reveal a word or phrase related to crime.

SCREEN MICE   _____

A CONSCIENCE
CITRIC FINES
HENS   _____

BOD LO   _____

ENACT UTOPIA   _____

EARLIER SKILLS   _____

AGE SHOT   _____

Answers on page 182.

MURDER
MYSTERY

Every word listed is contained within the group of letters. Words can be found in a straight line horizontally, vertically, or diagonally. They may be read either forward or backward.

ALIBI	MURDER
ARREST	MYSTERY
CORROBORATION	PLAN
ELIMINATE	PLANTED
EXONERATE	PROOF
LIES	SUSPECT
MOTIVE	SUSPICION

```
W C O R R O B O R A T I O N
E P L A N T E D Q R I I Q Q
I T R G P N O I C I P S U S
G L X E E K B C Q M F J W A
T G D C D E A U E I G O E O
C F M P P R X S M T U T L Z
E A H L R V U O Z U Z A I E
P M A E E O T M N W P V M V
S N S B H S O T J E Q N I I
U T I M R S L F P T R S N T
S X C B V I B I L A E A A O
X C T J P E T V A I X F T M
N T A F I D K R L U N A E E
Y C J O W S Y R E T S Y M B
```

Answers on page 182.

A COLORFUL
FLOWER

Cryptograms are messages in substitution code. Break the code to read the message. For example, THE SMART CAT might become FVO QWGDF JGF if F is substituted for T, V for H, O for E, and so on.

TCJ TNO QCZ BGNWF UNCGDN?

ZGDYNBZQC OCJMQ, FDGGZU

DI GJO NIAZGZO DI 1947. CZM

BJUX CNU BZZI WRQ DI CNGP.

QCZ HRMUZMZM TNO IZSZM

DUZIQDPDZU.

MURDER METHOD:
BEATS WITH A STICK

Change just one letter on each line to go from the top word to the bottom word. Do not change the order of the letters. You must have a common English word at each step.

BEATS

———

———

———

———

STICK

Answers on page 182.

THE MURDERER'S ITINERARY

The letters in ARIZONA can be found in boxes 2, 3, 5, 8, 14, and 16 but not necessarily in that order. Similarly, the letters in all the other cities and states can be found in the boxes indicated. Your task is to insert all the letters of the alphabet into the boxes. If you do this correctly, the shaded cells will reveal one more place that might be the murderer's location.

Hint: Compare TEXAS and SEATTLE to find the value of X, then TEXAS to BALTIMORE to find the value of S.

Unused letters: J and Q

ARIZONA: 2, 3, 5, 8, 14, 16

ATLANTA: 2, 3, 19, 23

BALTIMORE: 2, 5, 6, 8, 12, 14, 17, 19, 23

CHICAGO: 2, 5, 7, 8, 15, 20

CLEVELAND: 2, 3, 4, 6, 15, 22, 23

FLORIDA: 2, 4, 5, 8, 14, 21, 23

HOUSTON: 1, 3, 8, 11, 19, 20

MILWAUKEE: 2, 5, 6, 10, 11, 17, 18, 23

NEW YORK: 3, 6, 8, 10, 14, 18, 24

OAKLAND: 2, 3, 4, 8, 10, 23

PITTSBURGH: 1, 5, 7, 11, 12, 13, 14, 19, 20

SEATTLE: 1, 2, 6, 19, 23

ST. LOUIS: 1, 5, 8, 11, 19, 23

TEXAS: 1, 2, 6, 9, 19

1	2	3	4	5	6	7	8	9	10	11	12	13

14	15	16	17	18	19	20	21	22	23	24	25	26

UNUSUAL MURDER METHODS

Answer each question below about the words used for some unusual causes of death.

1. What word described throwing someone out a window?

    A. delectation

    B. defenestration

    C. dereliction

    D. deglutition

2. This word describes the act of burying someone alive.

    A. mortuarianism

    B. moratorium

    C. vivisection

    D. vivisepulture

3. This word describes sealing someone behind a wall, as in Edgar Allan Poe's "The Cast of Amontillado."

    A. enmeshment

    B. immurement

    C. inurnment

    D. internment

4. This word describes the draining of blood.

    A. exsanguination

    B. deslination

    C. deanimation

    D. evagination

Answers on page 182.

PICK YOUR
POISON

There are five bottles before you, but they've gotten jumbled up. Poison is found in one of them. If you arrange them from left to right, following the instructions given below, you will be able to know where the poison is found.

1. The poison is found in either the far left, middle, or far right positions.

2. The poison is found in neither the largest nor the smallest bottle.

3. The three medium-size sized bottles are found in a row.

4. At least one bottle separates the largest and smallest bottles.

THE CASE OF ED GEIN (PART I)

Read this true crime account, then turn to the next page to test your knowledge.

Ed Gein was the son of an overbearing mother. When she died in 1945, he was a 39-year-old bachelor living alone in a rundown farmhouse in rural Plainfield, Wisconsin. After his mother's death, he developed a morbid fascination with the medical atrocities performed by the Nazis during World War II. This fascination led him to dig up female corpses from cemeteries, take them home, and perform his own experiments on them, such as removing the skin from the body and draping it over a tailor's dummy.

He soon tired of decomposing corpses and set out in search of fresher bodies. Most of his victims were women around his mother's age. He went a step too far, however, when he abducted the mother of local sheriff's deputy Frank Worden. Learning that his missing mother had been seen with Gein on the day of her disappearance, Worden went to the Gein house to question the recluse. What he found there defied belief. Human heads sat as prize trophies in the living room along with a chair completely upholstered in human skin. But for Worden, the worst sight was in the woodshed. Strung up by the feet was the headless body of his mother. Her torso had been slit open, and her heart was horribly found on a plate in the dining room.

Gein confessed but couldn't recall how many people he'd killed. He told detectives that he liked to dress up in the carved-out torsos of his victims and pretend to be his mother. He spent ten years in an insane asylum before he was judged fit to stand trial. He was found guilty, but criminally insane, and died in 1984, at age 77.

THE CASE OF ED GEIN (PART II)

(Do not read this until you have read the previous page!)

1. Where did Ed Gein live?

    A. Plainfield, Wisconsin

    B. Plainfield, Michigan

    C. Whitfield, Wisconsin

    D. Springfield, Pennsylvania

2. How old was Gein when his mother died?

    A. 23

    B. 31

    C. 39

    D. 55

3. Gein died in this year.

    A. 1978

    B. 1977

    C. 1984

    D. He is still alive

Answers on page 182.

BUILDING BLUEPRINTS

Can you escape the scene of the murder? Start at the dot on the left and move to the right.

Answer on page 182.

THE MURDEROUS
GEM THIEF

5 types of gems were stolen from the murder scene. There was 1 gem of the first type, 2 of the second type, 3 of the third type, 4 of the fourth type, and 5 of the fifth type. From the information given below, can you tell how many gemstones of each kind were taken?

1. There are twice as many pearls as diamonds, but fewer pearls than pieces of jade.

2. Rubies are not the rarest gem.

3. There are an even number of sapphires.

4. Rubies are not the most plentiful gem.

Answers on page 182.   50

STILL UNSOLVED
135 YEARS LATER

Cryptograms are messages in substitution code.
Break the code to read the message. For example,
THE SMART CAT might become FVO QWGDF JGF if F
is substituted for T, V for H, O for E, and so on.

AF 1884, Z ONMAZD CADDNM

IMNVNU HF SHENF AF ZQOPAF,

PNTZO. JN SZO DZPNM FZENU

PJN ONMRZFP GAMD

ZFFAJADZPHM XV SMAPNM H.

JNFMV. JN CADDNU ZP DNZOP

ONRNF SHENF, ZFU HFN EZF, ZFU

AFBQMNU HPJNMO. JN SZO FNRNM

KHQFU. OHEN OINWQDZPNU

ZXHQP Z WHFFNWPAHF PH BZWC

PJN MAIINM.

Answers on page 182.

DID THE KILLER LEAVE A CLUE?

Change just one letter on each line to go from the top word to the bottom word. Do not change the order of the letters. You must have a common English word at each step.

KILL

———

———

———

———

———

———

———

CLUE

DNA SEQUENCE

Examine the two images below carefully. Are these sequences a match or not?

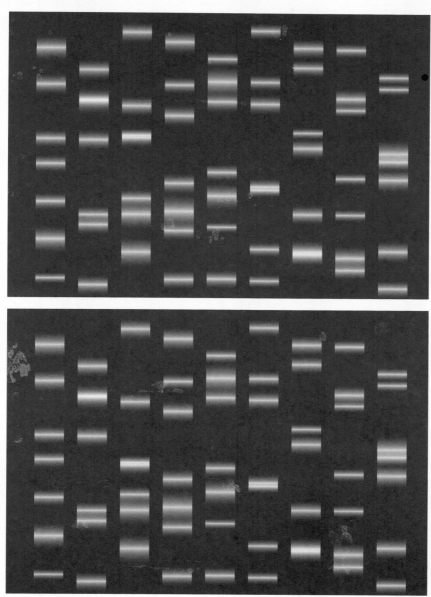

Answer on page 183.

A FICTIONAL CRIMINAL

Cryptograms are messages in substitution code. Break the code to read the message. For example, THE SMART CAT might become FVO QWGDF JGF if F is substituted for T, V for H, O for E, and so on.

GUR FPENAGBA FGENATYRE

VF GUR AVPXANZR SBE NA

HAFRRA FREVNY

PEVZVANY VA FPENAGBA,

CRAAFLYINAVN, BA GUR GI

FUBJ "GUR BSSVPR."

AN UNWANTED RECORD

Cryptograms are messages in substitution code. Break the code to read the message. For example, THE SMART CAT might become FVO QWGDF JGF if F is substituted for T, V for H, O for E, and so on.

ONX QHSOXP MOWOXM NWM

ONX NSANXMO HQFZXL IG

MXLSWE DSEEXLM, 76% IG

ONX TILEP'M OIOWE.

THE CASE OF CARL WANDERER (PART I)

Read this true crime account, then turn to the next page to test your knowledge.

In 1920, butcher Carl Wanderer—a veteran of World War I—approached a drifter in a bar and offered him the princely sum of $10 to pretend to rob him. Wanderer explained that he was in the doghouse with his wife, but that if he punched a mugger in front of her, he'd look like a hero. The drifter agreed to the deal.

The next day, as Wanderer and his wife (who was due to deliver the couple's first child the following month) returned home from the movies, the drifter attacked them in the entryway of their apartment building. Wanderer pulled out a gun, shot the drifter to death, then turned and shot his wife to death too. Wanderer told police that his wife had tragically been killed during the ruckus. For a couple of days, Wanderer was hailed as a hero. But police and newspaper reporters had an uneasy feeling about Wanderer's story. They were especially suspicious of the fact that he and the drifter had exactly the same model of pistol.

Reporters soon discovered that Wanderer had a girlfriend who worked across the street from Wanderer's butcher shop. Within weeks, Wanderer's story had fallen apart, and he broke down and confessed to the murders.

Initially put on trial only for the murder of his wife, Wanderer was sentenced to 25 years in prison. The newspapers were outraged that he hadn't been sentenced to hang and published the names and addresses of the jurors so that people could harass them. Eventually, Wanderer was rushed back into court to stand trial for the death of the drifter. This time, he was sentenced to death.

At his hanging, he entertained the reporters by singing a popular song of the day, "Old Pal Why Don't You Answer Me," just before his execution. One reporter said, "He shoulda been a song plugger." Another, however, said, "He should have been hanged just for his voice!"

THE CASE OF
CARL WANDERER (PART II)

(Do not read this until you have read the previous page!)

1. Wanderer was a veteran of this war.

   A. Civil War

   B. Spanish-American War

   C. World War I

   D. World War II

2. How much did Wanderer pay the drifter?

   A. 10 cents

   B. 1 dollar

   C. 10 dollars

   D. 25 dollars

3. What song did Wanderer sing before his execution?

   A. "Old Pal Why Don't You Answer Me"

   B. "For He's a Jolly Good Fellow"

   C. "Shoulda Been a Song Plugger"

   D. "It's a Long Way to Tipperary

Answers on page 183.

WHAT CHANGED? (PART 1)

Study this picture for one minute, then turn the page.

WHAT CHANGED? (PART II)

(Do not read this until you have read the previous page!)

Murder in the kitchen! From memory, can you tell what changed between this and the previous page to pinpoint what was used as a weapon?

PICK YOUR
POISON

There are five bottles before you, but they've gotten jumbled up. Poison is found in one of them. If you arrange them from left to right, following the instructions given below, you will be able to know where the poison is found.

1. The bottles are red, orange, yellow, green, and blue, but not necessarily in that order.

2. The poison is in a bottle with a primary color.

3. The yellow bottle is either in the middle or on the far right.

4. The blue bottle is either the far left bottle or the one next to it.

5. The orange bottle is to the immediate left of the bottle with the poison.

6. The red bottle is the furthest to the right.

7. The green bottle and the blue bottle are separated by one other bottle.

Answers on page 183.

MURDER METHOD: STABS WITH A SPEAR

Change just one letter on each line to go from the top word to the bottom word. Do not change the order of the letters. You must have a common English word at each step.

STABS

_____

_____

_____

_____

_____

_____

_____

_____

SPEAR

CRIME RHYMES

Each clue leads to a 2-word answer that rhymes, such as BIG PIG or STABLE TABLE. The numbers in parentheses after the clue give the number of letters in each word. For example, "cookware taken from the oven (3, 3)" would be "hot pot."

1. A blunt murder weapon found tucked inside a piece of footware (4, 4): _____ in the _____

2. A sharp murder weapon left behind in a grassy area in the woods (11, 5): _____ in the _____

3. A sharp murder weapon discarded in a sandy hill (7, 4): _____ in the _____

4. A blunt murder weapon kept in the cubicle of the video game maker (6, 10): _____ near the _____

5. A blunt murder weapon hidden in the bathroom (4, 3): _____ in the _____

6. A blunt murder weapon hidden in a piece of orna-mental pottery (4, 4): _____ in the _____

7. A strangling murder weapon found under your feet (4, 10): _____ under the _____

8. A sharp murder weapon left in a mesh kitchen device (4, 5): _____ in the _____

 Answers on page 183.

THE MURDEROUS GEM THIEF

5 types of gems were stolen from the murder scene. There was 1 gem of the first type, 2 of the second type, 3 of the third type, 4 of the fourth type, and 5 of the fifth type. From the information given below, can you tell how many gemstones of each kind were taken?

1. There are an even number of diamonds.

2. There are at least two pieces of topaz.

3. There are more rubies than sapphires.

4. There are three more rubies than there are pieces of turquoise.

5. There are more pieces of topaz than rubies.

Answers on page 183.

AN UNUSUAL CONFESSION

Cryptograms are messages in substitution code. Break the code to read the message. For example, THE SMART CAT might become FVO QWGDF JGF if F is substituted for T, V for H, O for E, and so on.

UAPY BAW QAPEGI HEIIAPQ RTPK

RDAJQAIUAQ EK. AS HAJMAP

VGIIAS RDA MLIEVA RL VLKBAQQ.

DA WGERAS GR G RAIAMDLKA

OLLRD RL OA MEVHAS TM.

A COMMON TERM

Cryptograms are messages in substitution code. Break the code to read the message. For example, THE SMART CAT might become FVO QWGDF JGF if F is substituted for T, V for H, O for E, and so on.

CMPKBP CAG QNBVGFJ FDBLR

PMABPR I. PBQQJBP (1937-2013) GQ

REB KFL VPBSGRBS WGRE VMGLGLD

REB RBPK "QBPGFJ IGJJBP" GL 1971.

Answers on page 183.

BLACK WIDOW
WORD SEARCH

Every word in all capitals below is contained within the group of letters. Words can be found in a straight line horizontally, vertically, or diagonally. They may be read either forward or backward.

CHICAGOAN TILLIE Klimek POISONED her husband, REMARRIED, and then did the same thing THREE more times, collecting life insurance and claiming that she'd FORESEEN her husbands' DEATHS in her DREAMS. Earning her the MONIKERS "Black WIDOW" and "Mrs. BLUEBEARD," Klimek is also SUSPECTED of having MURDERED a handful of her children, cousins, and a BOYFRIEND who didn't take the BAIT. She was SENTENCED to life in PRISON in 1922 and died in 1936.

```
M F E J W A D E T C E P S U S
Y O Z D Q X A E M X U M B M E
W R E N P P H E I T H L A O I
I E D E R J Z M O R U E J B L
D S E I I H C H X E R A K G L
O E R R S Q D H B D S A D W I
W E E F O Q E E I D B E M L T
P N D Y N U A B Y C C C J E F
O I R O N R T W A N A P T U R
P Q U B D Q H W E I Y G V M R
E F M J G O S T D H T Z O L C
J X C Q U O N J C E K B T A T
M O N I K E R S E X P R X J N
W E O P S U D E N O S I O P T
V Y B F N T H R E E I B T W C
```

Answers on page 183.

METHODS OF
MURDER

Unscramble each word or phrase below to reveal a murder method or tool.

I SNOOP _____

GNATS BIB _____

SOOTHING _____

BED LOUNGING _____

UH MENACING _____

RAGE TOR _____

HINGE STORM _____

WORN DING _____

GNARL STING _____

RAGGED _____

THE JENNINGS 8 (PART I)

Read this true crime account, then turn to the next page to test your knowledge.

The population of Jennings, Louisiana, is less than 10,000. This quiet parish seat of Jefferson Davis Parish was never known for much beyond its proximity to Louisiana's bayous. But then it became famous for the worst of reasons.

The first body was found floating in a canal on May 20, 2005. She was identified as 28-year-old Loretta Lynn Chaisson Lewis, who was known to engage in prostitution and drug use. Investigators were unable to determine a cause of death, but toxicology results revealed cocaine and alcohol in her system. Over the next four years, seven more women turned up dead. Sometimes the cause of death could not be determined, but at least two women were found with a slit throat.

At first, it seemed like the murders must have been the work of a serial killer, and police even had a suspect: a local strip club owner and drug dealer. But investigators were unable to piece together enough evidence to charge him with anything.

As the investigation continued, authorities were noticing many similarities between the eight victims. All of the women struggled with drug addiction, and all were from the south side of Jennings, known to be the home of the poorer working-class residents in the town. What's more, the victims all knew each other, some very well. And the women all shared another similarity: they were all police informants. The Jennings 8 families wonder if the women were "silenced" because of what they knew.

Ultimately, although four different people have been arrested in connection with the killings, the evidence has not been enough to support charges. The frustrated families believe that the women's lower socioeconomic standing, as well as their histories with drug use and prostitution, have quelled the authorities' interest in the case.

THE JENNINGS 8 (PART II)

(Do not read this until you have read the previous page!)

1. The first body was found in this year.

      A. 1998

      B. 2001

      C. 2003

      D. 2005

2. The victims came from this side of town.

      A. North

      B. South

      C. West

      D. East

3. Jennings is found in this area.

      A. Jefferson Davis parish, Louisiana

      B. Bayou, Louisiana

      C. Jennings, Georgia

      D. None of the above

Answers on page 184.

UNSOLVED IN THE NORTHEAST

Cryptograms are messages in substitution code. Break the code to read the message. For example, THE SMART CAT might become FVO QWGDF JGF if F is substituted for T, V for H, O for E, and so on.

BQ GWBPQ PWTWJ UKHWJ UWOW
FDGGWS EY QMW IKJJWIQDIRQ
ODTWO TBGGWY FDGGWO. QMW
FDGGWO, JWTWO DSWJQDXDWS,
RPWS PQBEEDJC BP MDP
HROSWO HWQMKS BJS
KLWOBQWS EWQUWWJ 1978 BJS
1987 EWXKOW PQKLLDJC.

Answers on page 184.

PICK YOUR
POISON

There are five bottles before you, but they've gotten jumbled up. Poison is found in one of them. If you arrange them from left to right, following the instructions given below, you will be able to know where the poison is found.

1. The teal bottle is to the right of the purple bottle, but not immediately to the right.

2. The red bottle is not next to the purple bottle.

3. The green bottle and the orange bottle are next to each other.

4. The orange bottle is next to the red bottle.

5. The poison is found in the bottle that is the second from the left.

WHAT HORRIBLE CRIMES!

Below is a group of words that, when properly arranged in the blanks, reveal a quote from Thomas De Quincey.

drinking incivility indulges little
murder once robbing Sabbath

If _____ a man _____ himself in

_____, very soon he comes to think

_____ of robbing; and from _____ he

comes next to _____ and

_____-breaking, and from that to

_____ and procrastination.

Answers on page 184.

ESCAPE FROM THE PARK

Can you escape from the murder scene? Start at the top left, and feel free to go under bridges.

Answer on page 184.

WILL THE JURY SET YOU FREE?

Change just one letter on each line to go from the top word to the bottom word. Do not change the order of the letters. You must have a common English word at each step.

JURY

———

———

———

———

———

———

———

FREE

Answers on page 184.

THE MURDERER'S ITINERARY

The letters in LONDON can be found in boxes 3, 10, 16, and 26, but not necessarily in that order. The same is true for the other cities listed below. Insert all the letters of the alphabet into the boxes. If you do this correctly, the shaded cells will reveal another city where the murderer might be.

Hint: Look for words that share a single letter. For example, ROME shares an O with SOFIA and an E with QUEBEC. By comparing the number lists following these 3 words, you can deduce the values of the 2 shared letters.

BRUSSELS: 7, 9, 18, 19, 21, 26

COPENHAGEN: 1, 3, 4, 5, 6, 16, 18, 24

HELSINKI: 1, 8, 9, 13, 16, 18, 26

JAKARTA: 2, 6, 7, 13, 20

LONDON: 3, 10, 16, 26

MEXICO CITY: 3, 4, 8, 15, 18, 20, 22, 23

QUEBEC: 4, 14, 18, 19, 21

QUEZON CITY: 3, 4, 8, 14, 15, 16, 17, 18, 19, 20

REYKJAVIK: 2, 6, 7, 8, 11, 13, 15, 18

ROME: 3, 7, 18, 23

SANTIAGO: 3, 6, 8, 9, 16, 20, 24

SOFIA: 3, 6, 8, 9, 12

VILNIUS: 8, 9, 11, 16, 19, 26

WARSAW: 6, 7, 9, 25

1	2	3	4	5	6	7	8	9	10	11	12	13

14	15	16	17	18	19	20	21	22	23	24	25	26

Cryptograms are messages in substitution code. Break the code to read the message. For example, THE SMART CAT might become FVO QWGDF JGF if F is substituted for T, V for H, O for E, and so on.

QBHU JHAHSHU ZWLUK ZPE

TVUAOZ PU QHPS MVY AOL

TBYKLY VM H ALLUHNL NPYS

BUAPS OPZ SHDFLY MVBUK

BUBZLK MVVAHNL MYVT

OIV'Z "JBYI FVBY

LUAOBZPHZT" AOHA WYVCLK

OL OHK ILLU HA H KVKNLYZ

NHTL DPAO OPZ ZPE-FLHY-

VSK KHBNOALY.

Answers on page 184.

DNA SEQUENCE

Examine the two images below carefully. Are these sequences a match or not?

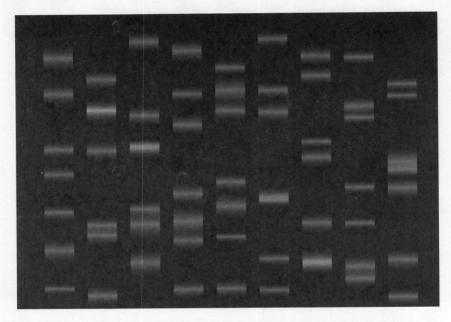

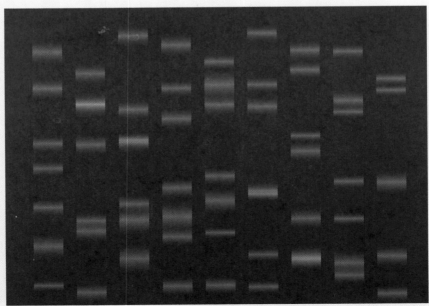

Answer on page 184.

THE MURDEROUS GEM THIEF

5 types of gems were stolen from the murder scene. There was 1 gem of the first type, 2 of the second type, 3 of the third type, 4 of the fourth type, and 5 of the fifth type. From the information given below, can you tell how many gemstones of each kind were taken?

1. There are an even number of opals.

2. There are an odd number of pearls.

3. There are more than two diamonds, but they are not the most plentiful gem.

4. There are half as many emeralds as rubies.

Answers on page 184.

JIMMY HOFFA

Every word listed is contained within the group of letters. Words can be found in a straight line horizontally, vertically, or diagonally. They may be read either forward or backward.

BRIBERY

CORRUPTION

DETROIT

GIACALONE

JUROR

JURY TAMPERING

LABOR

LEGALLY DEAD

MACHUS RED FOX

MAFIA

MICHIGAN

MOBSTER

ORGANIZED CRIME

PRISON

RESTAURANT

TEAMSTERS

UNION

UNSOLVED

WIRE FRAUD

```
C C M P R I S O N W D V G O
B L O J L U U S I E R I R C
R E B U H J L R T O A G X O
T G S R H N E R R C A T O R
E A T Y E F O U A N J N F R
A L E T R I J L I A Y A D U
M L R A T J O Z L G R R E P
S Y U M M N E N A I E U R T
T D O P E D S O B H B A S I
E E V E C W I I O C I T U O
R A T R X U S N R I R S H N
S D I I D G S U O M B E C P
O M Z N A I F A M L G R A L
E S W G U N S O L V E D M E
```

Answers on page 185.

MURDER METHOD: HITS WITH A CLUB

Change just one letter on each line to go from the top word to the bottom word. Do not change the order of the letters. You must have a common English word at each step.

HITS

____

____

____

____

____

____

____

____

CLUB

WHAT CHANGED?.
(PART I)

Study this picture for one minute, then turn the page.

WHAT CHANGED?
(PART II)

(Do not read this until you have read the previous page!)

Murder on the camping trip! From memory, can you tell what changed between this and the previous page to pinpoint what was used as a weapon?

PIOUS SOON ANAGRAMS

Unscramble each word or phrase below to reveal a poisonous substance.

RAINS _____

DOT EXTORTION _____

A ICY END _____

CHIN SENTRY _____

SIN CARE _____

MAMBO MAVEN _____

NO PIRATE _____

MAUL HILT _____

NEON BALLAD _____

HOCK ELM _____

I AID GILTS _____

RUE ARC _____

Answers on page 185.

BUILDING BLUEPRINTS

Navigate your way from top to bottom to escape the murder scene.

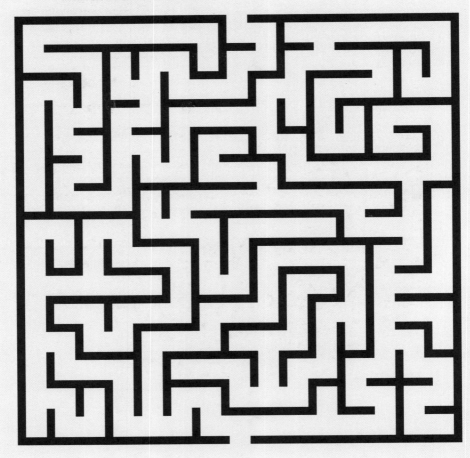

Cryptograms are messages in substitution code. Break the code to read the message. For example, THE SMART CAT might become FVO QWGDF JGF if F is substituted for T, V for H, O for E, and so on.

DON LEXNI RKN CDENSON

ZCIMRYVYQI SX MYVVOQO,

GYBUON KC K CESMSNO

RYDVSXO FYVEXDOOB GRSVO

KD CMRYYV, KXN COBFON KD

YXO ZYSXD KC KCCSCDKXD

NSBOMDYB YP DRO COKDDVO

MBSWO ZBOFOXDSYX

KNFSCYB MYWWSCCSYX.

Answers on page 185.

JACK GRAHAM

Every word listed is contained within the group of letters. Words can be found in a straight line horizontally, vertically, or diagonally. They may be read either forward or backward.

ALASKA	LUGGAGE
BOMB	MASS MURDER
CHECK FORGERY	MOTHER
DAISIE KING	PLANE
EXECUTION	SABOTAGE
EXPLOSION	SON
FBI	TRAVEL INSURANCE
FLIGHT	VANDALIZING
INHERITANCE	WRECKAGE

```
U E G A K C E R W B X R T P D
C E X D L V E C F B M Z R P C
U H C E G U H N O A G J A G E
E M E N C U G M A N X B V M X
A G S C A U B G I L U R E C P
B J A O K T T Z A P P E L F L
T U F T N F I I B G D H I B O
H Y A W O L O R O J E T N I S
G A H C A B Z R E N V O S D I
I O M D T X A T G H Q M U Y O
L N N R B U V S H E N I R X N
F A C F J L V L X P R I A M O
V N D A K A K S A L A Y N T G
P B D A I S I E K I N G C C A
R E D R U M S S A M J H E J A
```

Answers on page 185.

THE REDHEAD MURDERS (PART I)

Read this true crime account, then turn to the next page to test your knowledge.

In the 1980s, a string of murders of redheaded women along U.S. highways began to baffle investigators. It would take 30 years before any breaks would come in the cases, with one arriving from a very unlikely source.

On February 13, 1983, an elderly couple driving down Route 250 in Wetzel County, West Virginia, saw what they thought was a store mannequin lying in the snow. They soon realized, to their horror, that what they were seeing was not a plastic figure, but rather a dead body. The woman was white, about five feet six inches tall, and had brown eyes and reddish-brown auburn hair. Beyond those cursory characteristics, investigators were unable to identify her.

A year later, the body of a victim later identified as 28-year-old Lisa Nichols was found along Interstate 40 in West Memphis, Arkansas. She had been strangled to death, and like the Jane Doe found in West Virginia, had reddish hair. Over the next year, half a dozen more bodies were found along highways in Tennessee and Kentucky. Some of the victims were strangled or suffocated; some were too highly decomposed to determine a cause of death. Although they all shared a similar reddish hair color, the bodies were found hundreds of miles from each other and each case was handled by a different police department, so the connection wasn't immediately noted. Many of the victims seemed to be drifters without many family contacts. With no one searching for them or wondering about their fate, authorities weren't pressured to solve the cases.

Even though some began to consider the possibility of a serial killer early on, the

Redhead Murders (as they came to be known) were a low priority, eventually growing cold altogether. Until, that is, an unlikely group of investigators—a high school sociology class—began shining a new light on the murders. In 2018, students at Elizabethton High School in Tennessee studied the Redhead Murders for a class project, contacting police agencies and the FBI to create a profile of the likely killer or killers of the victims in each case. They concluded that the cases likely were connected, and the Redhead Murders were the work of a serial killer. Their profile theorized that the killer was a truck driver based in or near Knoxville, Tennessee, who would lure hitchhikers or prostitutes into his truck before killing them and dumping their bodies along the road.

Even more chilling is the fact that the killer in the Redhead Murder cases may have already been found. In 1985, a trucker named Jerry Leon Johns attempted to strangle a redheaded woman named Linda Schacke, throwing her on the side of Interstate 40 when he thought she was dead. Miraculously, Schacke survived the attack and Johns was arrested. Despite the obvious similarities to the Redhead Murders, he claimed to be innocent of the killings, and had airtight alibis that seemed to exclude him. But 30 years later, after Johns died in prison at the age of 67, his DNA was positively matched to one of the Redhead Murder victims. What's more, at the time of the killings, Johns lived in Cleveland, Tennessee, just southwest of Knoxville. Exactly as the students in the Elizabethton High School class had predicted.

Was Johns the Redhead Murder serial killer? We may never know for sure. But the story of the Redhead Murders investigation reminds us to never overlook a good idea or theory, even if it comes from the most unlikely source.

THE REDHEAD MURDERS (PART II)

(Do not read this until you have read the previous page!)

1. The first victim linked to the case was found in this state.

   A. Arkansas

   B. Kentucky

   C. Tennessee

   D. West Virginia

2. Students at this school proposed a compelling theory for the case.

   A. West Memphis High School

   B. Elizabethton High School

   C. Knoxville High School

   D. Wetzel County High School

3. This man was sent to prison for a 1985 attack on a redheaded woman.

   A. Jerry John Leon

   B. Jerry Leon Johns

   C. Jerry Leon Johnson

   D. Jerry John Leons

BLOOD AT THE SCENE

Change just one letter on each line to go from the top word to the bottom word. Do not change the order of the letters. You must have a common English word at each step.

BLOOD

_____

_____

_____

_____

_____

_____

_____

_____

SCENE

Answers on page 185.

PICK YOUR POISON

There are five bottles before you, but they've gotten jumbled up. Poison is found in one of them. If you arrange them from left to right, following the instructions given below, you will be able to know where the poison is found.

1. The poison is not found in the far left bottle or the bottle next to the far right bottle.

2. The red bottle is not next to the middle bottle.

3. The orange bottle is two bottles away from the bottle with the poison.

4. The green bottle is to the immediate left of the yellow bottle.

5. The blue bottle is immediately to the right of the red bottle.

6. The orange bottle is not found on either end.

BY THE NUMBERS

Below is a group of words that, when properly arranged in the blanks, reveal a quote from Beilby Porteus.

hero one millions villain

_____ murder made a _____:

_____ , a _____ .

SELF-JUSTIFICATION

Below is a group of words that, when properly arranged in the blanks, reveal a quote from Shakespeare's "Othello."

hate honor honorable murderer naught will

An _____ _____, if you _____

For _____ I did in _____, but all in _____ .

   Answers on pages 185-186.

DNA SEQUENCE

Examine the two images below carefully. Are these sequences a match or not?

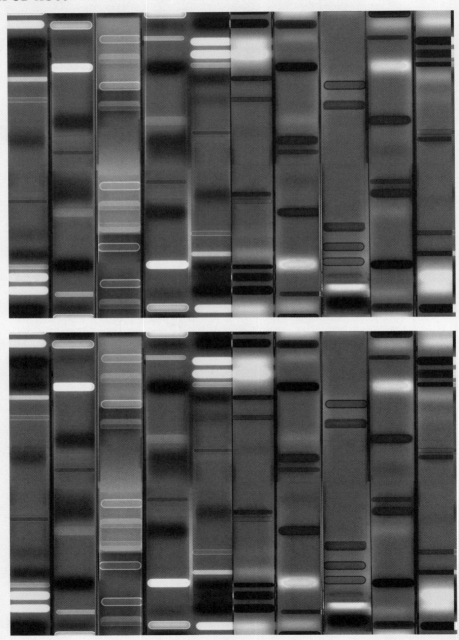

Answer on page 186.

MURDER METHOD:
SHOT BY GUNS

Change just one letter on each line to go from the top word to the bottom word. Do not change the order of the letters. You must have a common English word at each step.

SHOT

____

____

____

____

____

____

____

____

GUNS

Answers on page 186.

THE MURDEROUS
GEM THIEF

5 types of gems were stolen from the murder scene. There was 1 gem of the first type, 2 of the second type, 3 of the third type, 4 of the fourth type, and 5 of the fifth type. From the information given below, can you tell how many gemstones of each kind were taken?

1. There is one more garnet than amethyst.

2. There are at least two more peridots than diamonds.

3. Rubies are neither the most rare nor most plentiful gem.

4. There are more amethysts than diamonds.

5. There are two more garnets than rubies.

Answers on page 186.

BUILDING
BLUEPRINTS

Navigate the twisting path to flee the murder scene.

end

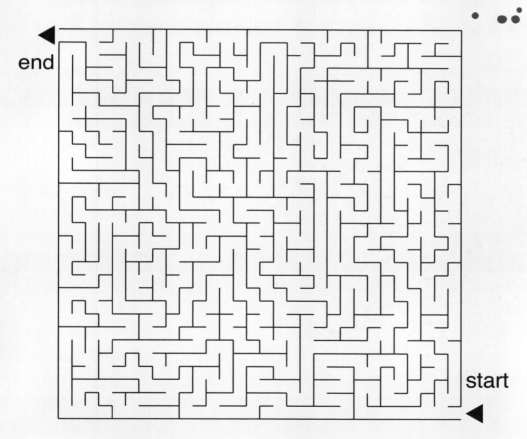

start

Answers on page 186.

CRIME...AND LOGIC

Cryptograms are messages in substitution code. Break the code to read the message. For example, THE SMART CAT might become FVO QWGDF JGF if F is substituted for T, V for H, O for E, and so on.

PJKLB KO PQLLQH.

ZQSKP KO JUJB.

NABJBEQJB KN KO TDQH

NAB ZQSKP JUNABJ NAUH

TDQH NAB PJKLB NAUN

RQT OAQTZC CFBZZ.

PICK YOUR POISON

There are six bottles before you, but they've gotten jumbled up. Poison is found in one of them. If you arrange them from left to right, following the instructions given below, you will be able to know where the poison is found. From left to right, the spots where the bottles can be placed are numbered 1, 2, 3, 4, 5, 6.

1. There are two blue bottles. They are not next to each other, and neither contains the poison.

2. The poison is in an even-numbered bottle.

3. The purple bottle is to the right of the yellow bottle, with at least two other bottles separating them.

4. The poison is in either the yellow bottle or the red bottle.

5. Both blue bottles are to the left of the purple bottle, which is not on either end.

6. The orange bottle is to the left of the red bottle, but not necessarily the immediate left.

7. The poison is not in a bottle with a number that can be divided by 3.

8. The orange bottle is to the right of one of the blue bottles.

Answers on page 186.

BURKE, HARE, KNOX

Every word listed is contained within the group of letters. Words can be found in a straight line horizontally, vertically, or diagonally. They may be read either forward or backward.

ANATOMY ACT	KNOX
ANATOMY CLASS	MARY DOCHERTY
BOARDING HOUSE	MEDICAL COLLEGE
BURKE	MURDER
CADAVERS	RESURRECTION MEN
DAFT JAMIE	
DISSECTION	SCOTLAND
EDINBURGH	SMOTHERED
HARE	TENANT

```
D R M A R Y D O C H E R T Y E A
I H E B H U T C Z E H Y O E S N
L S R S O A A V U N K B G M U A
B J S X U D R L T D J E D W O T
H H K A A R C E E D L O N N H O
S C N V L F R R L L V G A D G M
A E E L D C E E O B N O L D N Y
Z R I J M H Y C C O H B T K I A
S C D M T U L M I T U Z O N D C
O V W O A A R T O R I T C O R T
R E M W C J C D K T E O S X A X
M S B I O E T E E N A V N W O Y
Q Z D P S F I F A R C N J M B V
F E D S Y K S N A T X L A L E C
M L I G O Q T P J D O Y V C X N
M D F Y F C K E D I N B U R G H
```

Answers on page 186.

THE CASE OF AILEEN WUORNOS (PART I)

Read this true crime account, then turn to the next page to test your knowledge.

Aileen Wuornos was a confessed killer who shot at least seven men. But was she a cold-blooded murderer, or a victimized woman who was forced to defend herself?

By all accounts, Aileen Wuornos had a deeply troubled life right from the start. Born to teenaged parents on February 29, 1956, in Rochester, Michigan, she was the older of two siblings. She never met her father, who was in prison when she was born, serving time for child molestation. Just before Wuornos' fourth birthday, her mother abandoned her and her brother, leaving them with their grandparents.

It may have seemed like this arrangement would provide stability for Wuornos and her brother, but the truth was much less ideal. Although her grandparents legally adopted the siblings in 1960, they were

alcoholics and terrifyingly violent. Wuornos later stated that her grandfather sexually assaulted her and often beat her, and, after her grandmother died of liver failure in 1971, he threw her out of the house.

With nowhere to turn, Wuornos lived in the woods and relied on prostitution to support herself. She soon settled into a life of criminal activity, and was arrested numerous times for charges including theft, armed robbery, and disorderly conduct. She lived the life of a vagabond, eventually making her way to Florida, where she met and married a wealthy yacht club president named Lewis Fell in 1976. Wuornos caused trouble in their well-to-do neighborhood, where she was arrested for assault after starting a bar fight. She even attacked 69-year-old Fell with his own cane, prompting him to file a restraining order against her. Their marriage was annulled after only nine weeks.

Over the next decade, Wuornos perpetrated a string of crimes that spanned the Sunshine State, from armed robbery in Edgewater to forging checks in Key West. Then, in 1986, she met hotel maid Tyria Moore at a bar in Daytona Beach. The two began a relationship and moved in together, Wuornos continuing her work as a prostitute to support them.

In late 1989, Wuornos' prostitution work took a deadly turn. On November 30 that year, she had an encounter with 51-year-old Richard Charles Mallory, an electronics store owner from Clearwater. Police found Mallory's abandoned vehicle two days later, and on December 13, they discovered his body several miles away. He had been shot several times. Six more victims followed, all of them middle aged men who had been shot and left along the highway.

Witnesses began reporting two women, whose descriptions matched Wuornos and Moore, driving the victims' cars. After the pair abandoned one of the cars, police were able to lift fingerprints from it, which they matched to the two women. Wuornos and Moore were arrested, and Moore agreed to elicit a confession from her girlfriend in order to avoid prosecution.

Wuornos did confess to the crimes, but she claimed she had acted in self-defense. Mallory was a convicted rapist, so many of her supporters believed her claim that he violently attacked her and she was protecting herself; however, she was convicted of his murder and sentenced to death. She was also convicted of five other murders, and received six death sentences in total. She later provided a conflicting account of the killings, saying she murdered the men in order to rob them, not to defend herself, and said she "would kill again" if given the chance.

Wuornos was executed on October 9, 2002. Her life has been repeatedly depicted in documentaries, literature, songs, and, perhaps most famously, in the 2003 Oscar-winning film, *Monster*.

THE CASE OF
AILEEN WUORNOS (PART II)

(Do not read this until you have read the previous page!)

1. Wuornos was born in this state.

   A. Wisconsin

   B. Illinois

   C. Michigan

   D. Florida

2. During her brief marriage, Wuornos attacked her husband with:

   A. A knife

   B. A cane

   C. A pool cue

   D. A car

3. How many men is Wuornos alleged to have shot?

   A. Five

   B. Six

   C. Seven

   D. Eight

Answers on page 186.

WHAT CHANGED? (PART I)

Study this picture for one minute, then turn the page.

WHAT CHANGED? (PART II)

(Do not read this until you have read the previous page!)

Murder at the orchestra! From memory, can you tell what changed between this and the previous page to pinpoint what was used as a weapon?

Answers on page 186.

THE CASE OF ED KEMPER
(PART I)

Read this true crime account, then turn to the next page to test your knowledge.

Born in 1948, Edmund (Ed) Kemper was a tall man (6'9") with a genius IQ, but his appetite for murder took over at age 15 when he shot his grandparents because he wanted to see what it felt like. Nine years later, he had done his time for that crime, and during 1972 and 1973, Kemper hit the California highways, picking up pretty students and killing them before taking the corpses back to his apartment and then dissecting them. Nicknamed the "Co-ed Killer," he killed six women in that manner and then took an ax to his own mother, decapitating her, then using her body as a dartboard. Still not satisfied, he killed one of his mother's friends as well, and then fled from California to Colorado, anticipating an active manhunt that simple didn't happen.

Upset that his crimes didn't garner the media attention he thought they warranted, Kemper confessed to police. In fact, he confessed twice, as the first time he called from a phone booth and the police officer he spoke to didn't realize he was serious, telling him to call back later. Kemper did, and gleefully went into detail about his penchant for murder. He asked to be executed, but because capital punishment was suspended at the time, he got life imprisonment and remains incarcerated in California.

THE CASE OF ED KEMPER
(PART II)

(Do not read this until you have read the previous page!)

1. How tall was Ed Kemper?

    A. 6'6"

    B. 6'7"

    C. 6'8"

    D. 6'9"

2. Kemper operated out of this state.

    A. California

    B. Colorado

    C. Nevada

    D. Multiple states

3. Because he killed young students, Kemper acquired this nickname.

    A. The College Killer

    B. The University Ripper

    C. The Co-Ed Killer

    D. The Dorm Killer

Answers on page 186.

TO PUT IT BLUNTLY

Unscramble each word or phrase below to reveal an object that might be used for murder.

TICKS   _____

MAR HEM   _____

CRAB ROW   _____

NEW CHIPPER   _____

ATLAS BABBLE   _____

FLUB CLOG   _____

STITCH KING   _____

CUE POLO   _____

Answers on page 186.

THE MURDEROUS GEM THIEF

6 types of gems were stolen from the murder scene. There was 1 gem of the first type, 2 of the second type, 3 of the third type, 4 of the fourth type, 5 of the fifth type, and 6 of the sixth type. From the information given below, can you tell how many gemstones of each kind were taken?

1. There are even numbers of emeralds and sapphires.

2. There are odd numbers of pearls and pieces of jade.

3. There are more garnets than aquamarines, but garnets are not the most plentiful gem.

4. There are more aquamarines than pearls or pieces of jade.

5. There are more emeralds than sapphires.

6. There is more than one pearl.

THE MURDERER'S ITINERARY

The letters in UTAH can be found in boxes 4, 5, 15, and 26, but not necessarily in that order. Similarly, the letters in all the other states' names can be found in the boxes indicated. Insert all the letters of the alphabet into the boxes; if you do this correctly, the shaded cells will reveal a hidden state that might be the murderer's location.

Hint: Look for words that share a single letter. For example, OREGON shares an O with WASHINGTON and an R with NEBRASKA.

ARIZONA: 3, 4, 13, 19, 21, 22

CALIFORNIA: 3, 4, 7, 8, 19, 21, 22, 24

MAINE: 4, 11, 20, 21, 22

MICHIGAN: 4, 7, 15, 20, 21, 22, 23

NEBRASKA: 3, 4, 11, 12, 16, 22, 25

NEVADA: 4, 6, 9, 11, 22

NEW JERSEY: 2, 3, 11, 12, 17, 18, 22

NEW YORK: 3, 11, 17, 18, 19, 22, 25

OREGON: 3, 11, 19, 22, 23

PENNSYLVANIA: 4, 6, 8, 11, 12, 14, 18, 21, 22

TEXAS: 4, 10, 11, 12, 26

UTAH: 4, 5, 15, 26

WASHINGTON: 4, 12, 15, 17, 19, 21, 22, 23, 26

1	2	3	4	5	6	7	8	9	10	11	12	13
Q												
14	15	16	17	18	19	20	21	22	23	24	25	26

Answers on page 184.

A HAIR-RAISING MURDER

Cryptograms are messages in substitution code. Break the code to read the message. For example, THE SMART CAT might become FVO QWGDF JGF if F is substituted for T, V for H, O for E, and so on.

EH 1924, M TMLTGL MHZ

DEO SENG SGLG BECCGZ EH

TECCEHUO, FIHPMHM. PDGW

SGLG BECCGZ SEPD MH MV

PDGW BGJP NIL OJCEPPEHU

SIIZ. PDG BECCGL SMODGZ

DEO DMHZO EH PDG

TMLTGLODIJ SMODOPMHZ

MHZ CGNP, HGRGL PI TG

NIQHZ.

PICK YOUR POISON

There are six bottles before you, but they've gotten jumbled up. Poison is found in one of them. If you arrange them from left to right, following the instructions given below, you will be able to know where the poison is found.

1. The red bottle is somewhere to the left of the orange bottle but the right of the yellow bottle.

2. The blue bottle is not found on either end.

3. The poison is found in either the yellow bottle or a bottle on the end, but not both.

4. The poison is found in either the yellow bottle or a bottle with a color that yellow is used to make.

5. The green bottle is found to the left of the purple bottle, with three other bottles separating them.

6. The poison is not found in any bottle to the left of the blue bottle.

7. The red bottle separates the yellow and blue bottles.

8. The purple bottle is found directly next to the blue bottle.

   Answers on page 187.

BLACK WIDOW
WORD SEARCH

Every word in all capitals below is contained within the group of letters. Words can be found in a straight line horizontally, vertically, or diagonally. They may be read either forward or backward.

NORWEGIAN immigrant BELLE Poulsdatter, known as the Black WIDOW of the HEARTLAND was married for 17 years before her husband died and she collected $8,000 in life INSURANCE. Belle later married wealthy widower Peter GUNNESS who died when a meat GRINDER tumbled from a high shelf and landed on his head. His death was ruled accidental, and Belle collected Peter's insurance money and his ESTATE.

Belle advertised for FARMHANDS. Belle hired the ones who came with a sturdy BANK account as well as a STURDY back. LABORERS came and went—and some simply DISAPPEARED.

When the Gunness FARMHOUSE burned to the ground in 1908, the bodies of Belle's children and an unidentified headless female were found in the CELLAR. A search of the property revealed the bodies of Belle's suitors and laborers buried in the HOG pen, some killed by ARSENIC, some by skull TRAUMA. The widow was nowhere to be found. Belle's remaining BEAU and farmhand was convicted of murdering Belle and her family. However, the identity of the headless corpse was never conclusive, leading some to believe that Belle STAGED the entire thing and ESCAPED.

```
T I Y G R I N D E R R G A K V
B E L L E Q E E Z A L E R N Y
W M L Y N A V A L P S H S A D
S M E P J V J L B T A H E B D
K R D S L S E K A B M E N C E
F I E D U C T T C F U A I S R
B B N R T O E A P G A R C D A
W F E S O S H J G V R T R N E
U A A A U B S M G E T L H A P
R N H U U R A E R S D A S H P
H G T I V A A L N A V N T M A
D E P A C S E N U N F D U R S
G N T B A A R H C F U U R A I
N O R W E G I A N E T G D F D
D P H U R Z W O D I W F Y S N
```

Answers on page 187.

DID THE KILLER STEAL ANYTHING?

Change just one letter on each line to go from the top word to the bottom word. Do not change the order of the letters. You must have a common English word at each step.

KILLS

_____

_____

_____

_____

_____

_____   Seen in the sky or Hollywood

_____

_____

_____

_____   Sometimes precedes "wagon"

_____

_____

_____

_____

STEAL

Answers on page 187.

DNA SEQUENCE

Examine the two images below carefully. Are these sequences a match or not?

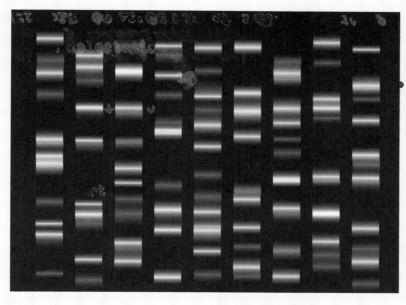

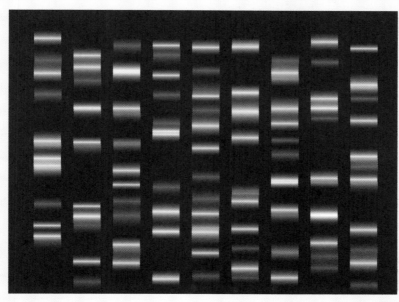

Answer on page 187.

THE CASE OF ONOPRIENKO
(PART I)

Read this true crime account, then turn to the next page to test your knowledge.

With nicknames like "The Beast of Ukraine" and "The Terminator," it's obvious that Soviet-Ukrainian Anatoly Yuryovych Onoprienko was not a model citizen. His reign of murderous terror only lasted six years, but in that short time he killed dozens of victims.

When Anatoly Yuryovych Onoprienko was finally apprehended, he told investigators that murdering people was pretty much his destiny. After all, according to statistics he'd read, around 70 percent of children who are brought up in orphanages grow up to engage in lives of crime. Onoprienko was one of those unlucky children; but surprisingly, he wasn't even an orphan.

Onoprienko was born on July 25, 1959, in the Ukrainian village of Lasky. He was the younger of two sons; his older brother, Valentin, was already 13 years old when he was born. When Onoprienko was four years old, his mother died. His grandparents began caring for him, even though his father, a decorated World War II veteran, was still alive. But soon after, Onoprienko's father turned him over to an orphanage, while the teenaged Valentin was free to continue living with their father. This may have been the beginning of a building resentment in the young Onoprienko.

Little is known about Onoprienko's younger adult life. It was not until 1989, when he was 30 years old, that he decided to carry out his first murder. And, unlike the tentative first crimes of some serial killers, he carried it out in terrifying fashion.

According to Onoprienko's confession, he enlisted the help of a friend, Sergei Rogozin, to break into a house with the intent of burglarizing it. But while they were robbing the house, the family of ten who lived there came home to find the intruders. Onoprienko and Rogozin killed all of them—two adults and eight children—using weapons they were carrying for "self-defense." After this first murder spree, Onoprienko cut ties with his friend and began working alone.

What followed was a string of murders from straight out of a nightmare. Onoprienko was deliberate in choosing his victims, searching for families who lived in isolated houses so there would be as few observers as possible. He would lure the occupants outside, or sometimes simply break down the door, then would systematically kill everyone in the home: first the male head of the household, followed by his wife, then lastly the children, who had just seen the horrifying murders of their parents. Onoprienko would then steal any valuables in the house before burning it down to destroy evidence. In several instances, he also killed random neighbors or people simply passing by, to eliminate the possibility of witnesses.

By 1996, police were alarmed by the number of unsolved murders in Ukrainian villages, and began to mobilize their forces in an effort to hunt down the killer. They eventually arrested a man named Yury Mozola, certain they had their murderer, and even tortured him in an effort to get him to confess. But Mozola refused to confess to anything, and ultimately died due to the brutal torture.

Several weeks later, Onoprienko was finally apprehended, discovered hiding out at his girlfriend's house. She was wearing a ring that he'd taken from one of his victims, and Onoprienko was in possession of a gun that was linked to many of the murders. Many investigators believe that Onoprienko's motives stemmed from his childhood abandonment. Perhaps the sight of happy families, something he never experienced, was more than he could bear. But Onoprienko offered another explanation, saying he was guided by "voices" who urged him to kill. Whatever the reason, "The Beast of Ukraine" would never again see freedom: the killer, who confessed to 52 murders, died in prison of heart failure in 2013, at the age of 54.

THE CASE OF ONOPRIENKO
(PART II)

(Do not read this until you have read the previous page!)

1. Onoprienko had a brother who stayed with their father, who was:

    A. Older than him

    B. Younger than him

    C. His twin

    D. Onoprienko had no brother.

2. In his first murder, Onoprienko and his friends killed:

    A. A family of four

    B. A family of six

    C. A family of eight

    D. A family of ten

3. Onoprienko's girlfriend had kept this piece of jewelry from a victim.

    A. Necklace

    B. Bracelet

    C. Ring

    D. Earrings

THE MURDEROUS
GEM THIEF

6 types of gems were stolen from the murder scene. There was 1 gem of the first type, 2 of the second type, 3 of the third type, 4 of the fourth type, 5 of the fifth type, and 6 of the sixth type. From the information given below, can you tell how many gemstones of each kind were taken?

1. Either there is one amethyst and six sapphires, or one sapphire and six amethysts.

2. There are an even number of diamonds.

3. There is either one more or one fewer emeralds than there are amethysts.

4. There are an odd number of pearls and rubies.

5. There are fewer pearls than diamonds.

     Answers on page 187.

THE GIGGLING
GRANDMOTHER

Every word in all capitals below is contained within the group of letters. Words can be found in a straight line horizontally, vertically, or diagonally. They may be read either forward or backward.

From the mid-1920s to the mid-'50s, Nannie DOSS left a trail of corpses: her MOTHER, two SISTERS, a NEPHEW, and a grandson. A mother of four trapped in an UNHAPPY marriage, Nannie also murdered two of her children with RAT poison before her first HUSBAND left her. She collected on the children's LIFE insurance policies. Nannie married three more times, but each husband contracted a MYSTERIOUS stomach AILMENT and died, leaving his widow his insurance SETTLEMENT, home, and estate.

Coincidentally, Nannie's fifth husband also died of a STOMACH ailment. His physician ordered an AUTOPSY, which showed a significant amount of rat POISON. After her arrest, the bodies of her former SPOUSES were EXHUMED for examination; all showed TRACES of poison. NANNIE giggled as she CONFESSED her crimes to the police, earning her the NICKNAME "The GIGGLING GRANDMOTHER."

```
P Q S X P W S E C A R T P K H
T N E M L I A Q S T T A R L U
X N I G U Y E E N P U Z L S S
S S W D R F S E O Y O A N I B
H U Y R I A M D P S U U G S A
R S O L E E N P E T S I S T N
H N X I L H A D O M G O M E D
P F E T R H T P M G U M D R S
C O T P N E S O L O N H A S N
V E I U H Y T I M E T D X K A
S D S S E E N S F O R H N E N
U H H D O G W L Y T B Z E I N
O Y F H T N H C A M O T S R I
L N I C K N A M E U M I R I E
T J R A D E S S E F N O C H E
```

Answers on page 188.

WHERE THE EVIDENCE LEADS US

Cryptograms are messages in substitution code. Break the code to read the message. For example, THE SMART CAT might become FVO QWGDF JGF if F is substituted for T, V for H, O for E, and so on.

TBCTXSVGFMGBFY UIBKUMTU

BV F IUCH GCBTJH GZBMQ. BG

SFH VUUS GW RWBMG IUCH

VGCFBQZG GW WMU GZBMQ, NXG

BD HWX VZBDG HWXC WLM

RWBMG WD IBUL F YBGGYU,

HWX SFH DBMK BG RWBMGBMQ

BM FM UPXFYYH

XMTWSRCWSBVBMQ SFMMUC GW

VWSUGZBMQ UMGBCUYH

KBDDUCUMG.

CRIME RHYMES

Each clue leads to a 2-word answer that rhymes, such as BIG PIG or STABLE TABLE. The numbers in parentheses after the clue give the number of letters in each word. For example, "cookware taken from the oven (3, 3)" would be "hot pot."

1. A blunt murder weapon left to dissolve in acid (3, 3): _____ in a _____

2. A blunt murder weapon left near a measuring device (5, 9): _____ behind the _____

3. A strangling weapon left behind in a transportation vehicle (5, 5): _____ in the _____

4. An explosive murder device left in a pile of tomatoes and eggplants (7, 11): _____ among the _____

5. A sharp murder weapon tossed near a type of tree (8, 8): _____ near the _____

6. A sharp murder weapon found in an airplane (7, 3): _____ in the _____

7. A poisonous murder weapon found where the boat is kept (7, 4): _____ on the _____

8. A sharp murder weapon displayed decoratively at the bar (5, 4): _____ above the _____

  Answers on page 188.

BUILDING BLUEPRINTS

Navigate the twisting path to get away from the murder scene.

start

end

SOLVE A CRIME

Change just one letter on each line to go from the top word to the bottom word. Do not change the order of the letters. You must have a common English word at each step.

CRIME

———

———

———

———

——— Opposite of losses, sometimes ill-gotten

———

———

———

——— To harass or attack, also a male name

———

———

———

———

———

———

SOLVE

Answers on page 188.

THE SON OF SAM (PART I)

Read this true crime account, then turn to the next page to test your knowledge.

Between July 1976 and July 1977, New Yorkers couldn't pick up a newspaper or turn on the television without hearing about the notorious serial killer who referred to himself in cryptic letters only as the Son of Sam. He struck seemingly at random, primarily attacking young women, and by the time he was finally captured on August 10, 1977, six people were dead and seven gravely wounded. The Son of Sam turned out to be a troubled loner named David Berkowitz, who told investigators upon his capture that demons in the form of howling dogs had instructed him to kill.

Abandoned as a baby, David was adopted by a middle-class couple who gave him a loving home. But Berkowitz grew up feeling scorned and unwanted because he was adopted. He made few friends, was viewed by neighbors as a bully, and did poorly in school. After his mother died and his father remarried, the animosity Berkowitz expressed toward his new stepmother eventually caused the newlywed couple to flee to Florida.

On Christmas Eve 1975, Berkowitz's internal rage reached the boiling point, and he stalked the streets with a knife, looking for someone to kill. He later told police that he stabbed two women that night, though police could locate only one, a 15-year-old girl named Michelle Forman who survived multiple stab wounds.

Berkowitz fled the Bronx and moved into a two-family home in Yonkers, where his mental state continued to decline. Barking dogs kept him awake at night, and Berkowitz eventually perceived their howls as demonic commands to kill. He moved out of the house and into a nearby apartment, where he became convinced that his neighbor's black Labrador Retriever was also possessed. After shooting the dog, Berkowitz came to believe that its owner also harbored demons.

The voices in his head eventually encouraged Berkowitz to once again seek victims on the street. On July 29, 1976, he shot Jody Valenti and Donna Lauria as they sat chatting in a car outside of Lauria's apartment. Lauria died instantly from a shot to the throat; Valenti survived. In the months that followed, Berkowitz continued his nocturnal attacks, using a distinctive .44 Bulldog revolver to dispatch his victims. He often shot couples. Some were killed, while others survived.

When he shot and killed both memebers of one couple on April 1, 1977, police found a rambling, handwritten letter from Berkowitz in which he referred to himself as "Son of Sam." In the note, Berkowitz revealed that he felt like an outsider and was programmed to kill. He told police that to stop his murderous rampage, they'd have to shoot him dead.

As the daily papers splashed gruesome details of each new killing across their front pages, New Yorkers began to panic. Women with dark hair cut their locks short or bought blond wigs because the killer seemed to have a penchant for brunettes. Many New Yorkers simply refused to go outside after dark.

A ticket for parking too close to a fire hydrant finally led to David Berkowitz's capture. On July 31, he had shot two people; the woman died while the man survived with visions loss. Two days later, a woman who lived near the murder scene called police to report seeing a strange man, later identified as Berkowitz, loitering in the neighborhood for several hours before snatching a parking ticket off the windshield of his car and driving away.

New York police detectives, working with the Yonkers police, decided to pay a visit to Berkowitz. They examined his car, parked outside his apartment, and spotted a rifle on the back seat. A search of the vehicle also revealed a duffel bag containing ammunition, maps of the crime scenes, and a letter to a member of the police task force charged with finding the Son of Sam.

Berkowitz was arrested later that evening as he started his car. He immediately confessed to being the Son of Sam, telling the arresting officers, "You got me. What took you so long?"

THE SON OF SAM (PART II)

(Do not read this until you have read the previous page!)

1. On what date was Berkowitz captured?

    A. July 31, 1976

    B. August 10, 1977

    C. April 1, 1977

    D. August 10, 1977

2. Berkowitz's neighbor had this type of dog.

    A. Golden Retriever

    B. Labrador Retriever

    C. German Shepherd

    D. Poodle

3. What kind of revolver did Berkowitz use?

_____

4. What did Berkowitz receive a ticket for shortly before his capture?

_____

WHAT CHANGED?
(PART I)

Study this picture for one minute, then turn the page.

WHAT CHANGED? (PART I)

(Do not read this until you have read the previous page!)

Murder by stabbing! From memory, can you tell what changed between this and the previous page to pin-point what was used as a weapon?

Answer on page 188.

ON THE
EDGE

Unscramble each word or phrase below to reveal an object that might be used for murder.

WORDS _____

TOY BANE _____

RAD EGG _____

TEACH EM _____

THE CHAT _____

ELK SIC _____

HE CYST _____

BATE MOCK FIN _____

Answers on page 188.

PICK YOUR POISON

There are six bottles before you, but they've gotten jumbled up. Poison is found in one of them. If you arrange them from left to right, following the instructions given below, you will be able to know where the poison is found.

1. The three primary colors, red, yellow, and blue, are all on the left, but not necessarily in that order.

2. The orange bottle is not on either end.

3. The blue bottle is separated from the purple bottle by three other bottles.

4. The yellow bottle is not next to the green bottle.

5. The red bottle is not next to the orange bottle.

6. Neither the blue bottle, the bottle on its left, nor the bottle on its right contain the poison.

7. Nor is the poison found in a bottle with a color that is made up of blue and another color.

8. The green bottle is separated from the purple bottle by one other bottle.

UNUSUAL MURDER METHODS

Answer each question below about some unusual causes of death.

1. These poisonous mushrooms are also called "death caps."
They resemble edible mushrooms like the straw mushroom.

    A. *Amanita phalloides*

    B. *Cantharellus cibarius*

    C. *Lentinula edodes*

    D. *Agaricus bisporus*

2. The cardiac medication Digoxin is derived from the plant
Digitalis, also known by this name. While it can be helpful,
digitalis can also be harmful.

    A. belladonna

    B. foxglove

    C. poinsettia

    D. larkspur

3. If you fed your enemy the liver of this animal, they might
die of vitamin A toxicity.

    A. stingray

    B. cod

    C. polar bear

    D. pig

4. Speaking of liver: serving the liver of this tetrodotox-
in-containing fish is banned in Japan.

    A. fugu

    B. saba

    C. ootoro

    D. unagi

Answers on page 189.

BLACK WIDOW
WORD SEARCH

Every word in all capitals below is contained within the group of letters. Words can be found in a straight line horizontally, vertically, or diagonally. They may be read either forward or backward.

Frank HILLEY had been married to MARIE for more than 20 years when he was admitted to the hospital with STOMACH pain and diagnosed with acute infectious HEPATITIS in 1975. He died within the month, and Marie collected on his life insurance POLICY. Three years later, she took out a life insurance policy on her DAUGHTER Carol, whereupon Carol developed a strange ILLNESS with SYMPTOMS of nausea and NUMBNESS in her extremities. Physicians detected an abnormal level of ARSENIC in Carol's system and suspected FOUL play. Frank's body was exhumed and TESTS revealed that he had died of arsenic POISONING.

Marie was ARRESTED in October 1979 for the attempted MURDER of her daughter, but was released on bond a month later. She promptly DISAPPEARED. Marie remained a fugitive for more than three years before marrying John Homan in FLORIDA under the ALIAS Robbi Hannon.

In a BIZARRE turn of events, Marie invented a TWIN sister, "Teri," staged "Robbi's" death, and then returned to her husband pretending to be her grief-stricken twin, Teri. The RUSE was discovered, and Marie was sent to Alabama, where she was wanted on other charges. She was convicted of murder and ATTEMPTED murder and sentenced to life in PRISON. Marie served four years of her sentence before she escaped during a FURLOUGH. She was found days later, freezing and wandering in the woods near Anniston, Alabama. Marie was admitted to the hospital, where she died of HYPOTHERMIA.

```
O C I N E S R A P R I S O N W
D D Y C I L O P G L G H T R M
G D E F F R S N S S N Y E J P
R D O T E L I A S B K P S D Q
H U I D P N O E I B L O T E S
L I R S O M N R I L F T S T I
P U L S A B E Z I U A H Y S T
M N I L M P A T R D F E M E I
V O I U E R P L T M A R P R T
P A N W R Y O E K A C M T R A
O V M E T U V F A R Z I O A P
R E T H G U A D Y R P A M F E
M I J H O M A R I E E K S F H
S T O M A C H Q Y B W D W H T
H Z B R U S E K I L L N E S S
```

Answers on page 189.

THE CASE OF CHARLES MANSON (PART I)

Read this true crime account, then turn to the next page to test your knowledge.

He is one of the most notorious criminals the country has ever seen. But surprisingly, although Charles Manson spent most of his life in prison, he never actually killed anyone with his own hands; he simply convinced others to do his bidding.

He was born Charles Milles Maddox on November 12, 1934, in Cincinnati, Ohio, to his 16-year-old mother, Kathleen Maddox. His biological father was nowhere to be found, so his mother married William Eugene Manson just before his birth. But his teenage mother wasn't ready to settle down with a baby and husband, and she often left her young son with various babysitters while she went out to binge drink. When Manson was five years old, his mother was arrested for assault and robbery, and spent the next three years in prison.

Manson was sent to live with an aunt and uncle until his mother's release from prison, then moved with her to West Virginia, where she continued to drink and run into trouble with the law. With such a tumultuous childhood, perhaps it's no surprise that Manson's first serious offense occurred when he was only nine years old. Known for his frequent truancy, the young Manson set his school on fire. This resulted in a stint at a boarding school for delinquent boys, which did nothing to stop his newfound criminal streak.

Over the next decade, Manson lived a life of lawlessness, first engaging in petty theft and then moving on to more serious offenses including car thefts and armed robberies. He received his first prison sentence—three years for stealing a car and failing to appear in court—in 1956. Another prison sentence followed in 1960, after Manson attempted to cash a forged check and then later took two women to New Mexico for the purpose of prostitution. While in prison, authorities noted that he had a "tremendous drive to call attention to himself."

When Manson was released from prison in 1967, he moved to San Francisco and rented an apartment with a female acquaintance. Over the next few months, he allowed more and more women to join them, until 19 women were living in the apartment with Manson. The group, often under the influence of LSD and other hallucinogenic drugs, considered him their "guru," and he began teaching his followers disturbing prophecies and implying that he was Jesus.

At he continued to gain followers, Manson moved "the Manson Family" to Spahn Ranch, a Los Angeles movie set that was no longer in use. He continued to prophesy to his followers, telling them that a race war would soon occur in the United States, and Armageddon was imminent. Even more unnerving, Manson began to believe that he was the key to unleashing the apocalypse.

Manson's plan was to purposely trigger the prophesied race war by killing white celebrities and pinning their murders on blacks. On August 8, 1969, he set his plan in motion. Four of Manson's followers were ordered to go to the house that actress Sharon Tate was renting, and to kill everyone inside. The resulting murders horrified the nation, as did the Manson-ordered murders of Leno and Rosemary LaBianca the next day.

Over the next few months, evidence pointing to many of Manson's Family members mounted, and on December 1, several of his followers were arrested. Manson was already in custody on suspicion of car theft, and the "guru" would never go free again. During the trial, neither Manson nor any of his followers showed remorse for their actions, and on January 25, 1971, Manson was convicted of first-degree murder and sentenced to death. His sentence would later be commuted to life in prison when California abolished the death penalty in 1972. The leader of the murderous Manson Family died on November 19, 2017, at the age of 83, having spent four decades behind bars.

THE CASE OF CHARLES MANSON (PART II)

(Do not read this until you have read the previous page!)

1. Manson was born in this state.

    A. California

    B. Ohio

    C. New Mexico

    D. West Virginia

2. Manson first went to prison in 1965 for this offense.

    A. Car theft

    B. Cashing a forged check

    C. Participating in crossing state lines for prostitution

    D. Drug use

3. Manson never killed someone in person, but directed murders.

    _____ True   _____ False

4. Manson's last name at birth was:

    A. Manson

    B. Maddox

    C. Spahn

    D. Milles

Answers on page 189.

WHAT CHANGED? (PART I)

Study this picture for one minute, then turn the page.

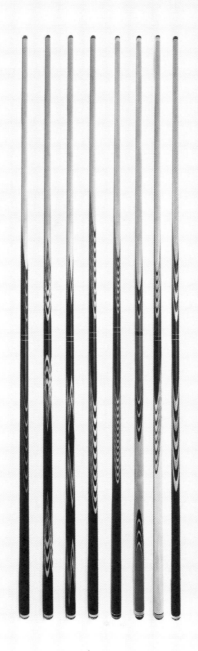

WHAT CHANGED? (PART II)

(Do not read this until you have read the previous page!)

Murder at the pool hall! From memory, can you tell what
changed between this and the previous page to pinpoint what
was used as a weapon?

Answer on page 186.

BUILDING BLUEPRINTS

Navigate the twisting path to escape from the murder scene.

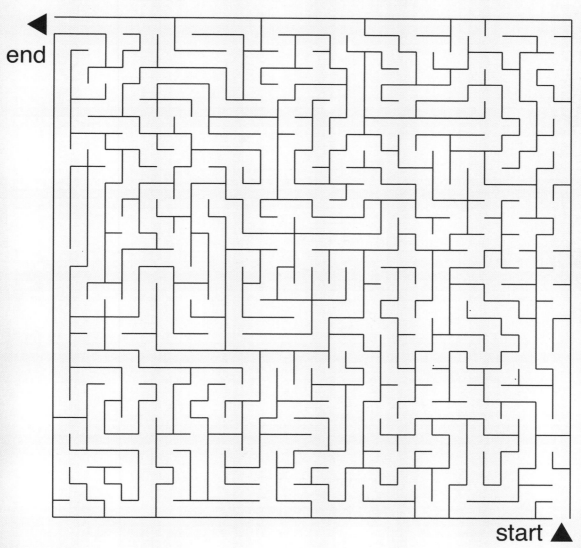

end

start ▲

Answer on page 189.

MURDER MYSTERIES

Change just one letter on each line to go from the top word to the bottom word. Do not change the order of the letters. You must have a common English word at each step.

MURDERS

_____   players or racehorses that do well on a wet, muddy field

_____   a perennial herb (plural form)

_____

_____

_____

_____

_____

_____

_____   those who read

_____

_____

_____

_____   baseball players

_____

_____

_____

MYSTERY

HOW IS A CRIMINAL BORN?

Cryptograms are messages in substitution code. Break the code to read the message. For example, THE SMART CAT might become FVO QWGDF JGF if F is substituted for T, V for H, O for E, and so on.

YXRTR WQ EA FTWUR WE

SEKAER'Q VPAAH SEK UATR

YXSE YXRTR WQ CAAHERQQ WE

YXR VPAAH AD AYXRTQ.

FTWUWESPQ STR EAY VATE.

YXRK STR USHR VK XJECRT,

NSEY SEH WELJQYWFR.

Answers on page 189.

DNA SEQUENCE

Examine the two images below carefully. Are these sequences a match or not?

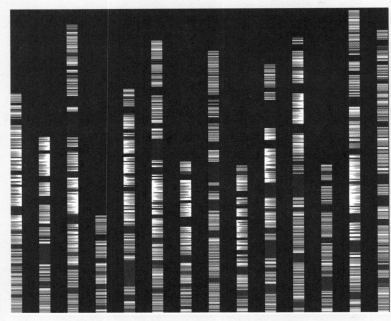

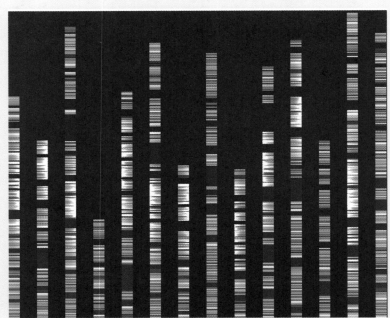

Answer on page 190.

THE WORST CRIMINAL

Cryptograms are messages in substitution code. Break the code to read the message. For example, THE SMART CAT might become FVO QWGDF JGF if F is substituted for T, V for H, O for E, and so on.

DH MHPI SWH QPVNNXQW

HPOZXQW UQQKCTSXVP SWUS

SWH KPHMKJUSHM UAH SWH

MUPOHAVKQ JAXCXPUZQ. DH

AHCHCNHA SWH AVCUP

HCTHAVAQ. DH AHCHCNHA SWH

OAHUS TVXQVPXPO TAXPJHQ

VG SWH AHPUXQQUPJH. DH QUI

SWUS SWH MUPOHAVKQ

JAXCXPUZ XQ SWH HMKJUSHM

JAXCXPUZ.

Answers on page 190.

THE MURDEROUS
GEM THIEF

7 types of gems were stolen from the murder scene. There was 1 gem of the first type, 2 of the second type, 3 of the third type, 4 of the fourth type, 5 of the fifth type, 6 of the sixth type, and 7 of the seventh type. From the information given below, can you tell how many gemstones of each kind were taken?

1. There are more than 4 pearls.

2. There are more diamonds than rubies, but fewer diamonds than amethysts.

3. There are twice as many peridots as emeralds.

4. There is exactly one more sapphire than there are rubies.

5. There is exactly one fewer pearl than there are amethysts.

6. There is one more peridot than there are emeralds.

Answers on page 190.

WAYS TO BEAT THE RAP

Unscramble each word or phrase below to reveal a word or phrase related to avoiding or evading a murder charge.

I BAIL
(1 word)

_____

FEARSOME OMEN
(2 words)

_____

FLEECE HUNT TORY
(3 words)

_____

LA GEL CYNICAL TITHE
(2 words)

_____

WARTY EAGLE
(3 words)

_____

OH THEY BIDED
(3 words)

_____

NEATEST WHOOPS
(3 words)

_____

ANEMIA HUTS
(3 words)

_____

Answers on page 190.

THE ZODIAC KILLER STRIKES (PART I)

Read this true crime account, then turn to the next page to test your knowledge. For another puzzle and the continuation of the story of the Zodiac Killer, see page 164.

On the evening of December 20, 1968, 17-year-old David Faraday and 16-year-old Betty Lou Jensen headed out on their first date in Benicia, California. Late that night, a passing motorist noticed two lifeless bodies lying next to a car at a "lover's lane" parking spot. It was Faraday and Jensen, who had both been shot to death. The unwitting couple became the first official victims of the Zodiac Killer, who would spend the next six years taunting the police and frightening the public.

The murders of Faraday and Jensen stumped investigators. There appeared to be no motive, and forensic data of the time yielded few clues. Why would someone gun down two teenagers who were merely out having fun? No leads developed, and the case quickly grew cold.

Months later, just before midnight on July 4, 1969, another young couple, Michael Mageau and Darlene Ferrin, were in their car at Blue Rock Springs Park in Vallejo, about four miles from where Faraday and Jensen were murdered. As they sat in the car, another car pulled up behind them and the driver exited, approaching their car with a flashlight. The stranger shined the bright light in their faces, and then, without warning, began shooting. When it was all over, Ferrin was dead; but Mageau, despite being shot three times, somehow survived.

About an hour later, at 12:40 a.m. on July 5, a man called the Vallejo Police Department saying he wanted to "report a murder," giving the dispatcher the location of Mageau and Ferrin's car. Using a calm, low voice, he also confessed that he had "killed those kids last year." It was the first contact anyone had with the killer, but it wouldn't be the last.

Mageau was able to describe his attacker as a white male with curly brown hair, around 200 pounds, 5 feet 8 inches tall, in his late 20s. It was little to go on, but it was a start. Then, on August 1, three Northern California newspapers, the "Vallejo Times Herald," "San Francisco Chronicle," and "San Francisco Examiner" all received virtually identical handwritten letters that contained crime details that only the killer could know. Each newspaper also received one third of a three-part coded cipher that the writer claimed would reveal his identity. The letters all ended with the same symbol: a circle with a cross through it.

The killer demanded that the ciphers be published on the front pages of each paper, otherwise he threatened to go on another killing spree. But investigators were not convinced that the letters came from the actual killer, so the "Chronicle" published its part of the code on page four, along with a quote from the Vallejo chief of police asking for more proof.

THE ZODIAC KILLER STRIKES
(PART II)

(Do not read this until you have read the previous page!)

For another puzzle and the continuation of the story of the Zodiac Killer, see page 164.

1. In what year did the Zodiac Killer first strike?

_____

2. The second victims of the Zodiac Killer, Mageau (who survived) and Ferrin (who was killed) were in the car at this park.

_____

3. The Zodiac Killer contacted this Police Department by phone after the second incident.

_____

4. Name the three California newspapers that received handwritten letters from the killer.

_____

_____

_____

WHAT CHANGED? (PART I)

Study this picture for one minute, then turn the page.

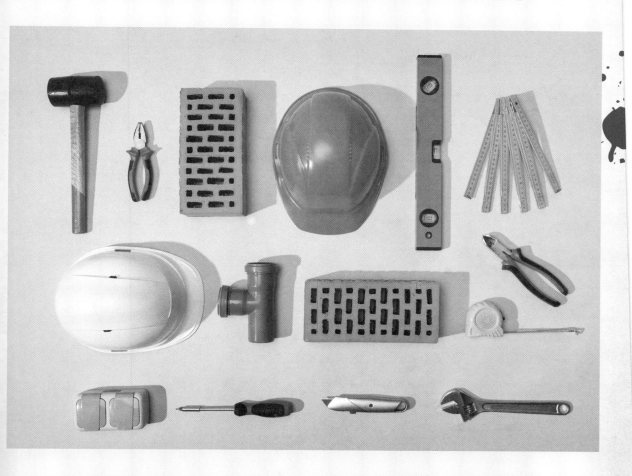

WHAT CHANGED? (PART II)

(Do not read this until you have read the previous page!)

Murder in the garage! From memory, can you tell what changed between this and the previous page to pinpoint what was used as a weapon?

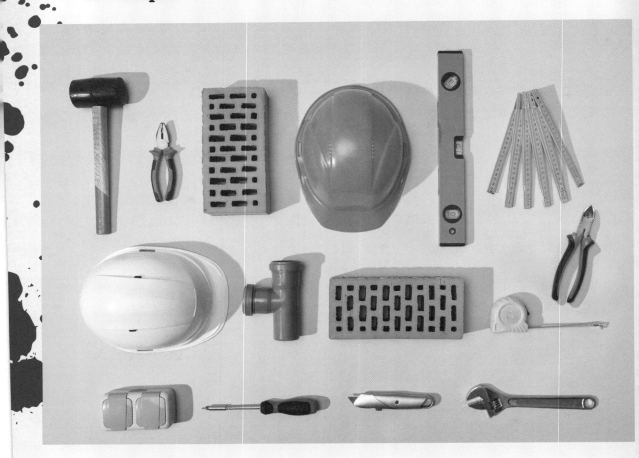

TO THE POINT

Unscramble each word or phrase below to reveal an object that might be used for murder.

HER BALD   _____

PARSE   _____

EVIL JAN   _____

ALE ROMP   _____

ROAN HOP   _____

VIE GAL   _____

TAN AGAIN   _____

LEA EXPO   _____

Answers on page 190.

VOLTAIRE
ON MURDER

Cryptograms are messages in substitution code. Break the code to read the message. For example, THE SMART CAT might become FVO QWGDF JGF if F is substituted for T, V for H, O for E, and so on.

XU XG SLERXYYNZ UL TXKK;

UJNENSLEN DKK IVEYNENG

DEN QVZXGJNY VZKNGG UJNO

TXKK XZ KDEFN ZVIRNEG DZY

UL UJN GLVZY LS UEVIQNUG.

MURDER AND STOLEN GEMS

The letters in ONYX can be found in boxes 6, 13, 19 and 22, but not necessarily in that order. Similarly, the letters in all the other valuables can be found in the boxes indicated. Your task is to insert all the letters of the alphabet into the boxes. If you do this correctly, the shaded cells will reveal two gem stones.

AQUAMARINE: 2, 4, 6, 7, 10, 11, 14, 25

BERYL: 4, 10, 12, 13, 17

CORAL: 2, 5, 10, 17, 22

EMERALD: 2, 3, 4, 10, 14, 17

FIRE OPAL: 2, 4, 10, 17, 20, 22, 23, 25

GARNET: 2, 4, 6, 10, 16, 18

IVORY: 9, 10, 13, 22, 25

JASPER: 1, 2, 4, 10, 21, 23

JEWELS: 1, 4, 17, 21, 26

KUNZITE: 4, 6, 8, 11, 15, 16, 25

ONYX: 6, 13, 19, 22

SAPPHIRE: 2, 4, 10, 21, 23, 24, 25

TOPAZ: 2, 15, 16, 22, 23

1	2	3	4	5	6	7	8	9	10	11	12	13

14	15	16	17	18	19	20	21	22	23	24	25	26

Answers on page 190.

H. H. HOLMES

Every word listed is contained within the group of letters. Words can be found in a straight line horizontally, vertically, or diagonally. They may be read either forward or backward.

BASEMENT

CHICAGO

COLUMBIAN
EXPOSITION

DEATH

DOCTOR

FINANCIAL SWINDLES

FRANK GEYER

FRAUD

HERMAN MUDGETT

MEDICAL SCHOOL

MURDER CASTLE

PHARMACIST

SECRET PASSAGEWAYS

SOCIOPATH

STOLEN CADAVERS

VAULT

WILMETTE

WORLD'S FAIR

```
E C C M W R M A U D E V H E S S
T H O S U H E D A F A V L O J Y
U E L E N R C Y H D Y K C N J A
L R U L C S D T E A O I H E L W
K M M D Y N A E N G O C T G N E
J A B N Y E K B R P K T T T A G
Y N I I D N P Q A C E N A O J A
M M A W W K E T X M A F A T R S
E U N S O W H K L Y Z S S R W S
D D E L X L L I G C Y I T O F A
I G X A D A W V I L C C R L N P
C E P I V X E O V A J L B K E T
A T O C A B C C M Y D A U R N E
L T S N U S C R E S S H L Y L R
S A I A L H A M F E K U O Y K C
C X T N T H X A M G W I F Z N E
H B I I P N I E P H B Z Y U T S
O N O F M R N V Z C H I C A G O
O X N D X T O U X G D U A R F H
L S T O L E N C A D A V E R S S
```

Answers on page 190.

DROWN IN THE WATER

Change just one letter on each line to go from the top word to the bottom word. Do not change the order of the letters. You must have a common English word at each step.

DROWN

_____
_____
_____
_____ cranky
_____
_____
_____
_____
_____
_____ supermodels have these
_____
_____
_____
_____
_____

WATER

Answers on page 191.   160

PICK YOUR POISON

There are seven bottles before you, but they've gotten jumbled up. Poison is found in one of them. If you arrange them from left to right, following the instructions given below, you will be able to know where the poison is found.

1. The bottles are red, orange, yellow, green, blue, purple, and pink. However, that order is not accurate at all. (That is, red is not on the far left, orange is not in the second space from the left, yellow is not in the third space, and so on; pink is not on the far right.)

2. Red and the colors that can be made with red by using blue, yellow, or white are grouped together, not necessarily in that order.

3. Blue is found on either the left or right end, with green immediately next to it.

4. The bottle in the middle contains the poison.

5. The yellow bottle is somewhere to the right of the pink bottle, but not on the far right end.

6. The orange bottle is on one side of the bottle with the poison.

7. The two colors that starts with "p" are next to each other in alphabetical order.

 Answers on page 191.

BUILDING BLUEPRINTS

Navigate the twisting path to escape the murder scene.

start ▼

end
◄

MOTIVES FOR
MURDER

Unscramble each word or phrase below to reveal a word or phrase that might compel someone to murder.

ACNE EN VEG   _____

EDGER   _____

HI NECTARINE   _____

ALACK LIMB   _____

RAFFIA   _____

HASTY CHOPPY   _____

SAY JOULE   _____

IFFY MAULED   _____

IMITATION DIN   _____

SHELTERING ILK   _____

Answers on page 191.

THE ZODIAC KILLER STRIKES AGAIN (PART I)

Read this true crime account, then turn to the next page to test your knowledge. (The first part of the story of the Zodiac Killer was found on page 150.)

The promised killing spree never materialized, and all three sections of the cipher were published over the next week. Then, on August 7, the "Examiner" received another letter that began with, "Dear Editor This is the Zodiac speaking." The killer now had a nickname which would soon become infamous. In the letter, the Zodiac Killer described details of the crimes known only to police, and taunted them for not yet solving his code, saying that once they did, they "will have me."

The very next day, a high school teacher named Donald Harden and his wife, Bettye, solved the cipher. The disturbing message began with the words "I like killing people because it is so much fun." The Zodiac then said that he was killing people to act as his "slaves" in the afterlife, in a rambling message full of misspellings and typos. But nowhere did the note reveal, or even hint, at the killer's identity.

On September 27, 1969, the Zodiac Killer struck again. A man wearing a black hood with a circle and cross symbol on his chest attacked college students Bryan Hartnell and Cecelia Shepard as they were picnicking at Lake Berryessa, tying them up and then stabbing them repeatedly. The attacker then drew the circle and cross symbol on Hartnell's car, along with the dates of each murder. Once again, he called the police—this time the Napa County Sheriff's Office—to report his own crime. And once again, the killer left behind a witness, when Hartnell survived the attack. Police were able to lift a palm print from the pay phone where the killer had called the police, but were unable to match it to a perpetrator.

Even with two witnesses, a description of the attacker, fingerprints, and handwritten letters, the identity of the Zodiac Killer remained frustratingly elusive. The last confirmed Zodiac Killer murder occurred on October 11, 1969, when he shot taxi driver Paul Stine in the head and then ripped off part of Stine's bloodstained shirt. The Zodiac Killer then sent another letter to the "Chronicle," along with a piece of Stine's shirt, in which he mocked police for failing to catch him and threatened to shoot school children on a bus.

Over the next few years, the Zodiac Killer kept up a strange correspondence with Bay Area newspapers, hinting at numerous other victims, making bomb threats, and demanding that people begin wearing buttons featuring his circle and cross symbol. Some of the letters included codes or strange references, including a 340-character cipher sent to the "Chronicle" on November 8, 1969, that has never been solved. He would often end his letters with a "score" claiming "SFPD = 0" while the Zodiac's "score" continued to climb, suggesting he continued his killing spree.

The final letter thought to be from the Zodiac Killer was sent on January 29, 1974; the killer then simply seemed to disappear. But the investigation into his identity continues to this day. More than 2,500 suspects have been considered—including the "Unibomber," Ted Kaczynski—but no one has ever been arrested. Law enforcement agencies hope that modern DNA testing may one day yield clues to his identity. Until then, the closing line of the Zodiac's final letter still haunts investigators: "Me - 37; SFPD - 0."

THE ZODIAC KILLER STRIKES AGAIN (PART II)

(Do not read this until you have read the previous page!)

1. The attack on September 27, 1969, took place at this location.

_____

2. Police lifted this from a pay phone.

_____

3. The Zodiac Killer sent his final letter in this month and year.

_____

4. The closing line of his last letter read:

_____

THE MURDEROUS
GEM THIEF

7 types of gems were stolen from the murder scene. There was 1 gem of the first type, 2 of the second type, 3 of the third type, 4 of the fourth type, 5 of the fifth type, 6 of the sixth type, and 7 of the seventh type. From the information given below, can you tell how many gemstones of each kind were taken?

1. There are fewer than 3 pieces of jade.

2. Diamonds are neither the most plentiful nor least plentiful gem.

3. There are an even number of topazes and an odd number of aquamarines.

4. There are twice as many rubies as sapphires, but not as many rubies as emeralds.

5. There are 3 more topazes than aquamarines.

6. There are more sapphires than aquamarines.

     Answers on page 191.

THE MOORS MURDERERS

Every word listed is contained within the group of letters. Words can be found in a straight line horizontally, vertically, or diagonally. They may be read either forward or backward.

ACIDIC SOIL

BURIED BODIES

DAVID SMITH

ENGLAND

GRISLY

IAN BRADY

KILLING SPREE

MANCHESTER

MOST HATED WOMAN

MURDER

MYRA HINDLEY

PHOTOGRAPHS

POLICE

PRISON

REMORSE

SADDLEWORTH MOOR

TWISTED

```
S L E L T T N Y U E B P Y M M
A M L E Y L S O R E H A S A Y
D S O T R N P M S O J E D N R
D H K S X P U O T I I K A C A
L O T Y T R S O L D R C V H H
E H P I D H G G O I I P F E I
W Y E E M R A B N D C M R S N
O T R D A S D T I I Y E R T D
R B W P N E D C E L L E P E L
T O H I I A S I S D M L A R E
H S B R S O L I V O W J I K Y
M D U A I T R G R A M O R K S
O B W L K G E S N O D Q M X R
O O B M B O E D U E X Z N A R
R M I A N B R A D Y C S M R N
```

Answers on page 191.

CRIME RHYMES

Each clue leads to a 2-word answer that rhymes, such as BIG PIG or STABLE TABLE. The numbers in parentheses after the clue give the number of letters in each word. For example, "cookware taken from the oven (3, 3)" would be "hot pot."

1. A sharp murder weapon hidden behind a DVD case for a romantic movie (3, 4; 5, 5): _____ _____ behind the _____ _____

2. A poisonous murder weapon left near the mantelpiece (7, 8): _____ by the _____

3. A projectile murder weapon hidden in the cabinet behind the fancy stemware (6, 7): _____ behind the _____

4. A blunt murder weapon found in an automobile (7, 3): _____ in the _____

5. An explosive murder weapon left in a tree (4, 4): _____ in the _____

6. A projectile murder weapon discarded in a device used to push small loads (5, 11): _____ in the _____

7. A smothering murder weapon tossed outside was found near this animal (6, 9): _____ near the _____

8. A sharp murder weapon thrown away in the pumpkin patch (5, 6): _____ among the _____

Answers on page 191.

WHAT CHANGED? (PART I)

Study this picture for one minute, then turn the page.

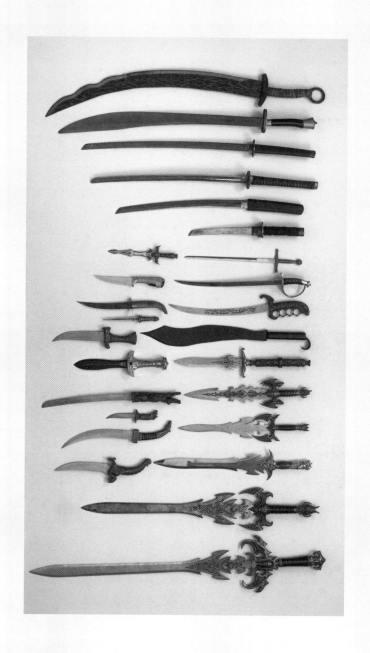

WHAT CHANGED? (PART II)

(Do not read this until you have read the previous page!)

Murder by stabbing! From memory, can you tell what changed between this and the previous page to pinpoint what was used as a weapon?

Answer on page 191.

MURDER
FROM AFAR

Unscramble each word or phrase below to reveal a word or phrase that might compel someone to murder.

SON LIGHTS   _____

OR WAR   _____

DOT BRAWL   _____

A SLOB   _____

ROB SCOWS   _____

OX NIGHTWEAR   _____

HIKE URNS   _____

SPOILT   _____

ERRED GRIN   _____

LOVER REV   _____

Answers on page 192.

ESCAPE THE
CORPORATE OFFICE

Navigate the twisting path to flee the office murder scene.

START

FINISH

MURDEROUS MAYHEM

A criminal mastermind who calls himself "Trixter" has hidden a stolen artifact in one of forty-five different safety deposit boxes at the local bank. Each box has a different number, and the miscreant has given the police a series of clues that will point to its hidden location. Using only these clues, find the one correct number—but be careful! Open the wrong box and the priceless artifact will be destroyed.

1. It is not divisible by 5.

2. The sum of the digits is 7, 9, or 11.

3. Both digits multiplied together is less than 10.

4. Both digits have the same number of letters.

51	52	53	54	55	56	57	58	59
41	42	43	44	45	46	47	48	49
31	32	33	34	35	36	37	38	39
21	22	23	24	25	26	27	28	29
11	12	13	14	15	16	17	18	19

Answers on page 192.

THE LINDBERGH KIDNAPPING

In 1932, the kidnapping of Charles Lindbergh, Jr., son of the famous aviator and his wife Anne, shocked the nation. Although a ransom was paid, the child was murdered. Bruno Richard Hauptmann was accused and convicted of the crime. Every word listed is contained within the group of letters. Words can be found in a straight line horizontally, vertically, or diagonally. They may be read either forward or backward.

ABDUCTION

ANNE MORROW

CARPENTER

CHARLES

CRIME OF THE CENTURY

GOLD CERTIFICATE

ELECTRIC CHAIR

EXECUTION

JOHN CONDON

KIDNAPPING

LADDER

LINDBERGH

RANSOM NOTE

RICHARD HAUPTMANN

```
E  C  G  Y  Q  J  P  J  G  N  I  E  B  N  E  R  D
S  R  J  K  H  Q  V  R  S  H  V  R  R  N  T  E  Y
D  I  U  I  D  N  X  K  X  K  O  A  C  A  A  D  K
Y  M  X  J  F  G  M  F  I  W  N  N  E  M  C  D  K
R  E  T  N  E  P  R  A  C  S  A  O  K  T  I  A  E
G  O  T  Z  G  U  H  U  O  B  D  D  D  P  F  L  L
N  F  I  S  N  R  U  M  D  N  E  N  A  U  I  J  E
I  T  G  E  X  E  N  U  I  K  J  O  N  A  T  C  C
P  H  Q  X  Z  O  C  Y  N  M  A  C  N  H  R  X  T
P  E  P  K  T  T  H  B  O  J  Q  N  E  D  E  B  R
A  C  J  E  I  C  A  H  I  V  X  H  M  R  C  M  I
N  E  T  O  X  Y  R  V  T  B  H  O  O  A  D  O  C
D  N  N  R  V  E  L  W  U  H  J  J  R  H  L  K  C
I  T  L  I  H  R  E  D  C  Z  R  J  R  C  O  G  H
K  U  V  J  U  V  S  A  E  Q  Q  O  O  I  G  F  A
N  R  M  N  U  N  B  U  X  W  H  Y  W  R  M  T  I
T  Y  C  A  R  H  G  R  E  B  D  N  I  L  X  Z  R
```

Answers on page 192.

BUILDING BLUEPRINTS

Navigate the twisting path to get away from the murder scene.

start

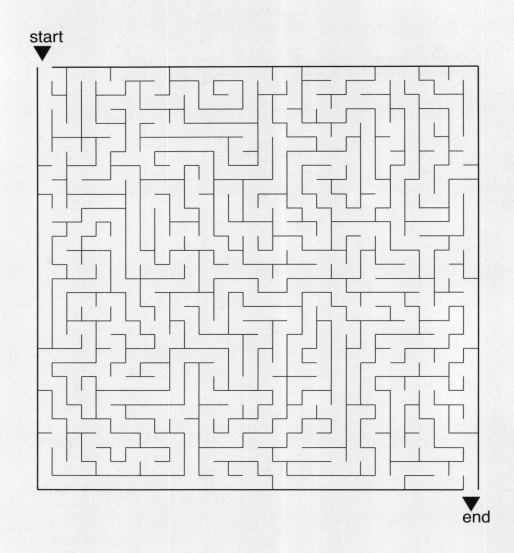

end

ANSWERS

DNA Sequence (page 4)

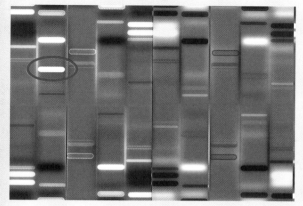

Criminal Anagrams (page 5)

Arrested; warrant; locked away; inmates; prison; Rikers Island

Se7en (pages 6-7)

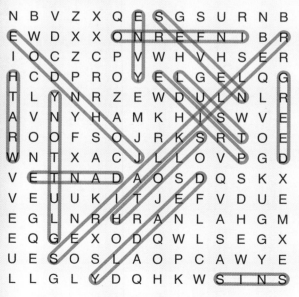

Crime Cryptogram (page 8)

The Golden State Killer committed at least 13 murders between 1974 and 1986.

Crime Cryptogram (page 8)

What is the pseudonym for an unidentified American serial killer? Zodiac.

What Changed? (pages 9-10)

The cap on the bottle on the left disappeared.

Crime Rhymes (page 11)

1. bludgeon in the dungeon; 2. knife in the fife; 3. rifle behind the trifle; 4. guns in the buns; 5. pipe wrapped in pinstripe; 6. wrench under a bench; 7. wire in the mire; 8. rope behind the telescope

Pick Your Poison (page 12)

From left to right, the bottles are green, blue, red, and yellow. The poison is found in the red bottle.

The Case of Harold Shipman (pages 13-14)

1. C. 1970–1998; 2. A. £386,000; 3. A. Heroin

Escape by Train (page 15)

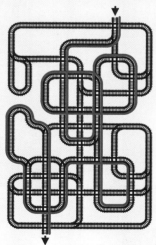

ANSWERS

Will the Killer Go to Jail? (page 16)
Answers may vary. KILL, fill, fall, fail, JAIL; KILL, mill, mall, mail, JAIL

Will the Killer Go Free? (page 16)
Answers may vary. KILL, fill, fell, feel, feet, fret, FREE

Zodiac Killer Cryptogram (page 17)
On August 1, 1969, three Northern California newspapers, the Vallejo Times Herald, San Francisco Chronicle, and San Francisco Examiner all received virtually identical handwritten letters that contained crime details that only the killer could know. Each newspaper also received one third of a three-part coded cipher that the writer claimed would reveal his identity. The letters all ended with the same symbol: a circle with a cross through it.

A Grim Vision (page 18)
O world, no world, but mass of public wrongs, Confused and filled with murder and misdeeds.

To Murder or Not to Murder (page 18)
O! my offense is rank, it smells to heaven; It hath the primal eldest curse upon 't, A brother's murder!

The Murderer's Itinerary (page 19)

1	2	3	4	5	6	7	8	9	10	11	12	13
G	S	W	I	T	Z	E	R	L	A	N	D	H

14	15	16	17	18	19	20	21	22	23	24	25	26
P	Y	Q	K	U	J	X	C	V	B	M	O	F

An Alarming Statistic (page 20)
In almost 15% of serial murder cases, the victims are chosen entirely at random.

Count to Four (page 20)
What are the four types of homicide? Capital Murder, Murder, Manslaughter, and Criminally Negligent Homicide

Pick Your Poison (page 21)
From left to right, the bottles are purple, yellow, red, and green. The poison is found in the purple bottle.

Making a Murderer (pages 22-23)

The Murderous Gem Thief (page 24)
The count is: 1 emerald, 2 rubies, 3 sapphires, 4 diamonds, 5 pearls.

ANSWERS

The Most Famous Unsolved Case (pages 25–26)

1. A. Mary Ann Nichols; 2. C. Mary Kelly; 3. C. 1880s

Escape from the Park (page 27)

Quotes on a Theme (page 28)

Truth will come to light; murder cannot be hid long.
—Shakespeare, "The Merchant of Venice"
Murder, though it have no tongue, will speak with most miraculous organ.
—Shakespeare, "Hamlet"
Murder will out.
—Cervantes, "Don Quixote"
Mordre wol out, certeyn, it wol nat faille.
—Chaucer, "The Canterbury Tales"

Murder Method: Hit with a Pipe (page 29)

Answers may vary. HITS, pits, pips, PIPE. 6-step variant: HITS, sits, sins, wins, wine, wipe, PIPE

Murder Method: Hit with a Pool Cue (page 29)

Answers may vary. HIT, hut, cut, CUE

DNA Sequence (page 30)

They are a match.

What Changed? (pages 31–32)

A knife in the bottom right corner now faces the other way.

Colorful Crime (page 33)

"Amber Alerts" are messages that go out to the public every time a child goes missing.

Crime Cryptogram (page 33)

Who were the hillside stranglers? Angelo Buono Jr. and Kenneth Bianchi.

Pick Your Poison (page 34)

From left to right, the bottles are blue (1), yellow, blue (2), green. The poison is found in the yellow bottle.

Romance Gone Wrong (page 35)

Answers may vary. KISS, miss, mist, mint, mind, mild, mill, KILL

One Way to End a Marriage (page 36)

There is nothing more dread and more shameless than a woman who plans such deeds in her heart as the foul deed which she plotted when she contrived her husband's murder.

A Noisy Crime (page 36)

Other sins only speak; murder shrieks out.

The Case of Andrei Chikatilo (page 37–38)

1. D. The Rostov Ripper; 2. C. 55; 3. A. Rope and butcher knife

ANSWERS

Criminal Anagrams (page 39)

Crime scene; forensic science technicians; blood; caution tape; serial killers; hostage

Murder Mystery (pages 40-41)

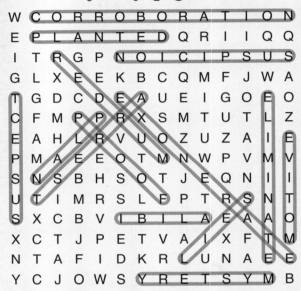

A Colorful Flower (page 42)

Who was the Black Dahlia? Elizabeth Short, killed in Los Angeles in 1947. Her body had been cut in half. The murderer was never identified.

Murder Method: Beats with a Stick (page 43)

Answers may vary. BEATS, seats, sears, stars, stark, stack, STICK

The Murderer's Itinerary (page 44)

1	2	3	4	5	6	7	8	9	10	11	12	13
S	A	N	D	I	E	G	O	X	K	U	B	P
14	15	16	17	18	19	20	21	22	23	24	25	26
R	C	Z	M	W	T	H	F	V	L	Y	J	Q

Unusual Murder Methods (page 45)

1. B. defenestration; 2. D. vivisepulture;
3. B. immurement; 4. A. exsanguination

Pick Your Poison (page 46)

From left to right, the bottles are: largest, medium, medium, medium, smallest. The poison is found in the middle, medium-size bottle.

The Case of Ed Gein (pages 47-48)

1. A. Plainfield, Wisconsin; 2. C. 39; 3. C. 1984

Building Blueprints (page 49)

The Murderous Gem Thief (page 50)

The count is: 1 diamond, 2 pearls, 3 rubies, 4 sapphires, and 5 pieces of jade.

Still Unsolved 135 Years Later (page 51)

In 1884, a serial killer preyed on women in Austin, Texas. He was later named the servant girl annihilator by writer O. Henry. He killed at least seven women, and one man, and injured others. He was never found. Some speculated about a connection to Jack the Ripper.

ANSWERS

Did the Killer Leave a Clue? (page 52)
Answers may vary. KILL, bill, bell, belt, bolt, bout, gout, glut, glue, CLUE

DNA Sequence (page 53)

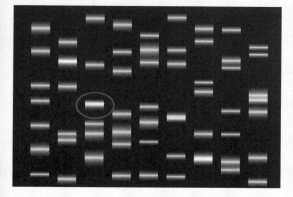

A Fictional Criminal (page 54)
The Scranton Strangler is the nickname for an unseen serial criminal in Scranton, Pennsylvania, on the TV show "The Office."

An Unwanted Record (page 54)
The United States has the highest number of serial killers, 76% of the world's total.

The Case of Carl Wanderer (pages 55–56)
1. C. World War I; 2. C. 10 dollars; 3. A. "Old Pal Why Don't You Answer Me"

What Changed? (pages 57–58)
The meat fork disappeared.

Pick Your Poison (page 59)
From left to right, the bottles are orange, blue, yellow, green, and red. The poison is found in the blue bottle.

Murder Method: Stabs with a Spear (page 60)
Answers may vary. STABS, stars, stare, stale, stall, shall, shell, shelf, sheaf, shear, SPEAR

Crime Rhymes (page 61)
1. rock in the sock; 2. switchblade in the glade; 3. harpoon in the dune; 4. hammer near the programmer; 5. club in the tub; 6. mace in the vase; 7. cord under the floorboard; 8. shiv in the sieve

The Murderous Gem Thief (page 62)
The count is: 1 turquoise, 2 diamonds, 3 sapphires, 4 rubies, and 5 pieces of topaz.

An Unusual Confession (page 63)
Very few serial killers turn themselves in. Ed Kemper called the police to confess. He waited at a telephone booth to be picked up.

A Common Term (page 63)
Former FBI Special Agent Robert K. Ressler (1937–2013) is the man credited with coining the term "serial killer" in 1971.

Black Widow Word Search (pages 64–65)

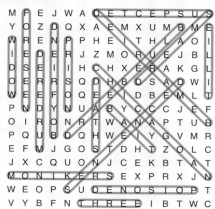

ANSWERS

Methods of Murder (page 66)
Poison; stabbing; shooting; bludgeoning; machine gun; garrote; smothering; drowning; strangling; dagger

The Jennings 8 (pages 67-68)
1. D. 2005; 2. South; 3. A. Jefferson Davis parish

Unsolved in the Northeast (page 69)
At least seven women were killed by the Connecticut River Valley killer. The killer, never identified, used stabbing as his murder method and operated between 1978 and 1987 before stopping.

Pick Your Poison (page 70)
From left to right, the bottles are purple, green, orange, red, and teal. The poison is found in the green bottle.

What Horrible Crimes! (page 71)
If once a man indulges himself in murder, very soon he comes to think little of robbing; and from robbing he comes next to drinking and Sabbath-breaking, and from that to incivility and procrastination.

Escape from the Park (page 72)

Will the Jury Set You Free? (page 73)
Answers may vary. JURY, bury, busy, bust, best, beat, feat, feet, fret, FREE

The Murderer's Itinerary (page 74)

1	2	3	4	5	6	7	8	9	10	11	12	13
H	J	O	C	P	A	R	I	S	D	V	F	K

14	15	16	17	18	19	20	21	22	23	24	25	26
Q	Y	N	Z	E	U	T	B	X	M	G	W	L

Unusual Exoneration (page 75)
Juan Catalan spend six months in jail for the murder of a teenage girl until his lawyer found unused footage from HBO's "Curb Your Enthusiasm" that proved he had been at a Dodgers game with his six-year-old daughter.

DNA Sequence (page 76)

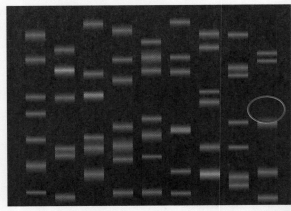

The Murderous Gem Thief (page 77)
The count is: 1 emerald, 2 rubies, 3 diamonds, 4 opals, and 5 pearls.

ANSWERS

Jimmy Hoffa (pages 78-79)

Murder Method: Hits with a Club (page 80)

Answers may vary. HITS, sits, sets, sees, seed, feed, fled, flee, flue, clue, CLUB

What Changed? (pages 81-82)

The pocket knife disappeared.

Pious Soon Anagrams (page 83)

Sarin; tetrodotoxin; cyanide; strychnine; arsenic; mamba venom; atropine; thallium; belladonna; hemlock; digitalis; curare

Building Blueprints (page 84)

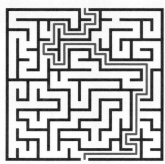

A Blameless Cover (page 85)

Ted Bundy had studied psychology in college, worked as a suicide hotline volunteer while at school, and served at one point as assistant director of the Seattle Crime Prevention Advisory Commission.

Jack Graham (pages 86-87)

The Redhead Murders (pages 88-90)

1. D. West Virginia; 2. B. Elizabethton High School; 3. B. Jerry Leon Johns

Blood at the Scene (page 91)

Answers may vary. BLOOD, blond, blind, blink, blank, plank, plant, slant, scant, scent, SCENE

Pick Your Poison (page 92)

From left to right, the bottles are red, blue, orange, green, and yellow. The poison is found in the yellow bottle.

By the Numbers (page 93)

One murder made a villain, millions, a hero.

ANSWERS

Self-Justification (page 93)
An honorable murderer, if you will;
For naught I did in hate, but all in honor.

DNA Sequence (page 94)
They are a match.

Murder Method: Shot by Guns (page 95)
Answers may vary. SHOT, shop, stop, step, stem, seem, sees, sets, gets, guts, GUNS

The Murderous Gem Thief (page 96)
The count is: 1 diamond, 2 rubies, 3 amethysts, 4 garnets, and 5 peridots.

Building Blueprints (page 97)

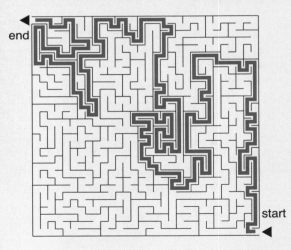

Crime...and Logic (page 98)
Crime is common. Logic is rare. Therefore it is upon the logic rather than upon the crime that you should dwell. — Sir Arthur Conan Doyle, "The Adventure of the Copper Beeches"

Pick Your Poison (page 99)
From left to right, the bottles are blue (1), yellow, blue (2), orange, purple, and red. The poison is found in the yellow bottle.

Burke, Hare, Knox (pages 100-101)

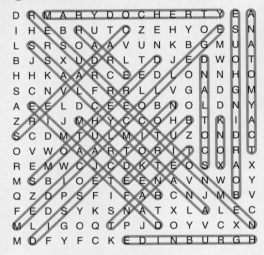

The Case of Aileen Wuornos (pages 102-104)
1. C. Michigan; 2. B. A cane; 1. C. 7

What Changed? (pages 105-106)
The flute disappeared.

The Case of Ed Kemper (pages 107-108)
1. D. 6'9"; 2. A. California; 3. C. The Co-Ed Killer

To Put It Bluntly (page 109)
Stick; hammer; crowbar; pipe wrench; baseball bat; golf club; nightstick; pool cue

ANSWERS

The Murderous Gem Thief (page 110)

The count is: 1 piece of jade, 2 sapphires, 3 pearls, 4 aquamarines, 5 garnets, and 6 emeralds.

The Murderer's Itinerary (page 111)

1	2	3	4	5	6	7	8	9	10	11	12	13
Q	J	R	A	U	V	C	L	D	X	E	S	Z

14	15	16	17	18	19	20	21	22	23	24	25	26
P	H	B	W	Y	O	M	I	N	G	F	K	T

A Hair-Raising Murder (page 112)

In 1924, a barber and his wife were killed in Billings, Montana. They were killed with an ax they kept for splitting wood. The killer washed his hands in the barbershop washstand and left, never to be found.

Pick Your Poison (page 113)

From left to right, the bottles are green, yellow, red, blue, purple, and orange. The poison is found in the orange bottle.

Black Widow Word Search (pages 114-115)

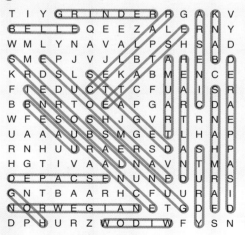

Did the Killer Steal Anything? (page 116)

Answers may vary. KILLS, bills, bells, sells, seals, sears, stars, stark, stack, stuck, shuck, chuck, check, cheek, cheer, sheer, steer, steel, STEAL

DNA Sequence (page 117)

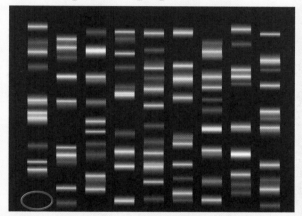

The Case of Onoprienko (pages 118-120)

1. A. Older than him; 2. D. A family of ten; 3. C. Ring

The Murderous Gem Thief (page 121)

The count is: 1 amethyst, 2 emeralds, 3 pearls, 4 diamonds, 5 rubies, and 6 sapphires.

ANSWERS

The Giggling Grandmother (pages 122–123)

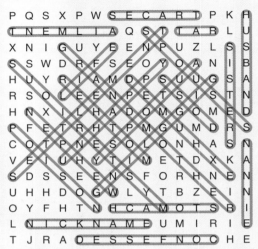

Where the Evidence Leads Us (page 124)

Circumstantial evidence is a very tricky thing. It may seem to point very straight to one thing, but if you shift your own point of view a little, you may find it pointing in an equally uncompromising manner to something entirely different. — Arthur Conan Doyle, "The Adventures of Sherlock Holmes"

Crime Rhymes (page 125)

1. bat in a vat; 2. brick behind the yardstick; 3. chain in the train; 4. grenade among the nightshades; 5. stiletto near the palmetto; 6. bayonet in the jet; 7. hemlock on the dock; 8. spear above the beer

Building Blueprints (page 126)

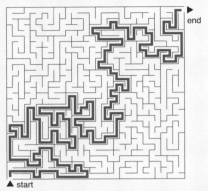

Solve a Crime (page 127)

Answers may vary. CRIME, grime, gripe, grips, grins, gains, pains, pairs, hairs, hairy, harry, carry, curry, curvy, curve, carve, calve, salve, SOLVE

The Son of Sam (pages 128–130)

1. D. August 10, 1977; 2. B. Labrador Retriever; 3. .44 Bulldog; 4. Parking near a fire hydrant

What Changed? (pages 131–132)

An extra knife was snuck into the collection!

On the Edge (page 133)

Sword; bayonet; dagger; machete; hatchet; sickle; scythe, combat knife

Pick Your Poison (page 134)

From left to right, the bottles are yellow, blue, red, green, orange, and purple. The poison is found in the orange bottle.

ANSWERS

Unusual Murder Methods (page 135)

1. A. *Amanita phalloides*; 2. B. foxglove; 3. C.polar bear; 4. A. fugu

Black Widow Word Search (pages 136-137)

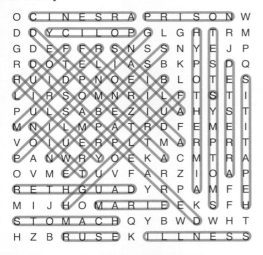

The Case of Charles Manson (pages 138-140)

1. B. Ohio; 2. A. Car theft; 3. True; 4. B. Maddox

What Changed? (pages 141-142)

Two pool cues swapped places.

Building Blueprints (page 143)

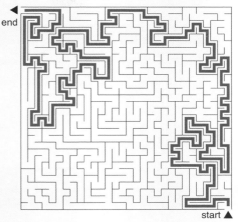

Murder Mysteries (page 144)

Answers may vary. MURDERS, mudders, madders, ladders, larders, warders, wanders, ganders, genders, renders, readers, headers, heaters, beaters, betters, batters, matters, masters, mastery, MYSTERY

How Is a Criminal Born? (page 145)

There is no crime in anyone's blood any more than there is goodness in the blood of others. Criminals are not born. They are made by hunger, want and injustice. — Khuswant Singh, Train To Pakistan

ANSWERS

DNA Sequence (page 146)

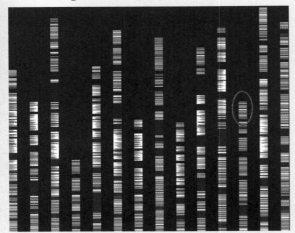

The Worst Criminal (page 147)

We deny the snobbish English assumption that the uneducated are the dangerous criminals. We remember the Roman Emperors. We remember the great poisoning princes of the Renaissance. We say that the dangerous criminal is the educated criminal. — G. K. Chesterton, The Man Who Was Thursday

The Murderous Gem Thief (page 148)

The count is: 1 emerald, 2 peridots, 3 rubies, 4 sapphires, 5 diamonds, 6 pearls, and 7 amethysts.

Ways to Beat the Rap (page 149)

Alibi; frame someone; flee the country; legal technicality; get a lawyer; hide the body; toss the weapon; use a hitman

The Zodiac Killer Strikes (pages 150-152)

1. 1968; 2. Blue Rock Springs Park; 3. Vallejo; 4. "Vallejo Times Herald," "San Francisco Chronicle," and "San Francisco Examiner"

What Changed? (pages 153-154)

The set of pliers rotated.

To the Point (page 155)

Halberd; spear; javelin; pole arm; harpoon; glaive; naginata; pole axe

Voltaire on Murder (page 156)

It is forbidden to kill; therefore all murderers are punished unless they kill in large numbers and to the sound of trumpets. — Voltaire

Murder and Stolen Gems (page 157)

1	2	3	4	5	6	7	8	9	10	11	12	13
J	A	D	E	C	N	Q	K	V	R	U	B	Y
14	15	16	17	18	19	20	21	22	23	24	25	26
M	Z	T	L	G	X	F	S	O	P	H	I	W

H. H. Holmes (pages 158-159)

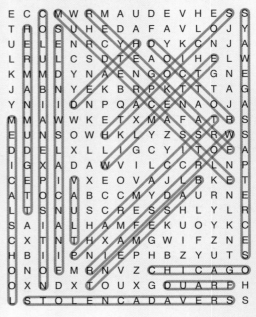

ANSWERS

Drown in the Water (page 160)

Answers may vary. DROWN, grown, grows, gross, cross, crops, chops, chaps, chats, coats, costs, posts, poses, loses, loves, lover, liver, liter, later, WATER

Pick Your Poison (page 161)

From left to right, the bottles are pink, purple, orange, red, yellow, green, and blue. The poison is found in the red bottle.

Building Blueprints (page 162)

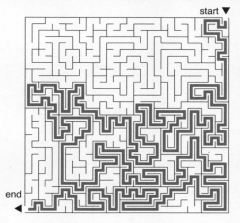

Motives for Murder (page 163)

Vengeance; greed; inheritance; blackmail; affair; psychopathy; jealousy; family feud; intimidation; thrill seeking

The Zodiac Killer Strikes Again (pages 164–166)

1. Lake Berryessa; 2. Palm print; 3. January 1974; 4. Me – 37; SFPD – 0.

The Murderous Gem Thief (page 167)

The count is: 1 aquamarine, 2 pieces of jade, 3 sapphires, 4 topazes, 5 diamonds, 6 rubies, and 7 emeralds.

The Moors Murderers (pages 168–169)

Crime Rhymes (page 170)

1. ice pick behind the chick flick; 2. cyanide by the fireside; 3. pistol behind the crystal; 4. crowbar in the car; 5. bomb in the palm; 6. arrow in the wheelbarrow; 7. pillow near the armadillo; 6. sword among the gourds

What Changed? (pages 171–172)

A curved knife on the left changed direction.

ANSWERS

Murder from Afar (page 173)

slingshot; arrow; blowdart; bolas; crossbow; throwing axe; shuriken; pistol; derringer; revolver

Escape the Corporate Office (page 174)

Murderous Mayhem (page 175)

The answer is 16.

The Lindbergh Kidnapping (pages 176–177)

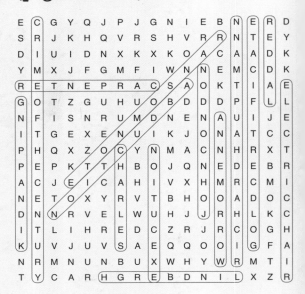

Building Blueprints (page 178)

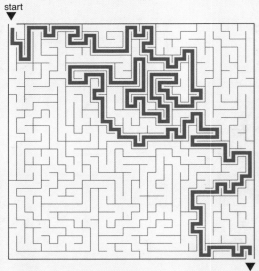

start

end